365 DAYS OF VEGAN RECIPES

Emma Katie

Check out more books by Emma Katie at:
www.amazon.com/author/emmakatie

Contents

Introduction 1

Chapter 1: Appetizers: 3

Southwestern Style Mini Tortilla Pizzas 4
Spinach Vegan Puff-Pastry Strudel 4
Vegan Green Quesadillas 5
Easy Mean White Bean Dip 5
Bean and Carrot Spirals 6
Asian-Inspired Summer Goi Cuan 6
Very Vegan Crunchy Chile Nachos 7
Yummy Roasted Mushrooms 7
Tofu Nuggets with Barbecue Glaze 8
Savory Scallion Pancakes 8
Broiled Japanese Eggplants 8
Smokin' Peanut and Tofu 9
Groovy Indian Samosas 9
Artichoke Attack Appetizer 10
Vegan Creation Coleslaw 11
Lucky Lemon Mushrooms 11
Finger-Licking Appetizer Pretzels 11
No-Egg Deviled Tomatoes 12
Quick-Fix Cashew and Date 12
No-Meat Pre-Dinner Meatballs 13
Autumnal Roasted Chestnuts 13
Indian Garbanzo Beans 14
Finger-Licking' Spiced Crackers 14
Tempeh Finger Fries 15
Everyday Cantankerous Kale Chips 15
Freedom Sweet Fries 15
Baby Finger Burgers 16
Mediterranean Garbanzo-Bean Fritters 16
Super Rad-ish Avocado Salad 17
Beauty School Ginger Cucumbers 17

Chapter 2: Dipping Sauces and Spreads 19

Romesco Sauce 20
Sun-Dried Tomato with Black Olive Flair Spread 20
Summertime Garlic Bean Dip 21
Spicy Lovin' Bean Dip 21
Natural-Variety Cilantro Black Bean Dip 21

Sun-Dried Sunny Tomato Tofu Dip 22
Turkish-Based Beet Muhummara Spread 22
Green Pistachio Pesto 22
Parsley Pea Pesto 23
Tofu Spinach Dip 23
Potatoes with Almond-Based Pesto 24
Faux Chopped Liver 24
Greek Tofu Tahini Dip 24
Eggplant and Tahini Mediterranean Spread 25
Tangy Artichoke-Based Roasted Eggplant Dip 25
Chermoula Dipping Sauce 26
Ultimate Vegan Hummus 26
Summertime Tomato Guacamole 27
Mean Bean Salsa 27
Tropical Pineapple Chunky Salsa 27
Vegetable-Based Guacamole 28
Super Spicy Green Salsa 28
El Avocado Mambo Mango Salsa 29
Tomatillo and Yellow Corn Dip 29

Chapter 3: Vegan Cheese Recipes 31

Good Gouda Vegan Cheese 32
What a Breeze Vegan Brie Cheese 32
"Cheddar Cheese" Vegan Spread 33
Herb is the Word Vegan Cheese 33
Pesto Tofu Cheese Spread 34
Texas Smoked Cheddar Cheese 34
Rad Vegan Ricotta 34
Eggplant-Based Vegan Queso 35
Vegan Blue Cheese Dressing 35
Vegan Mayonnaise 36
Flaxseed-Based Mayonnaise 36
Cashew-Based Vegan Sour Cream 37
Cashew-Based Vanilla Yogurt 37
New Day Vegan Mozzarella Cheese 38
Vegan Swiss Cheese 38
Vegan Thousand Island Dressing 39
Vegan Buttercream Frosting Recipe 39

Chapter 4: Vegan for the Kids 41

Vegan Baby Cereal 42
Vegan Baby Rice Cereal 42
Baby's Barley Cereal 42
Too-Fun Tofu Fajitas 43
McDonald's Enemy Tofu Chicken Nuggets 43

No-Cheese Mac-N-Cheese..43
Fruit and Faux Yogurt Morning Parfait 44
Children's Corn Chowder 44
Tempting Tofu Chocolate Pudding 45
Winter Weather Tofu Scallops..45
Sweet Carolina French Fries 46
Groovy Pizza Pie Potatoes 46
Macaroni Veggie-Loving Salad for Kids 47
Raising a Raisin Carrot Salad 47
Picnic Ready Vegan Potato Salad 47
Homemade Joyous Kid-Friendly Peanut Butter 48
Magic Morning Blueberry Muffins 48
School Lunch Vegan Wrap..49
School Lunch Onion and Tempeh Wrap 49
Vegan Groovy Elvis Sammie 49
No-Egg, Yes-Way Egg Salad 50
Kiddie Quinoa Sloppy Joe 50

Chapter 5: Start Your Morning Right: Very Vegan Breakfast Recipes 53

Super Vegan Pancakes with Pine Nut-Inspired Maple Syrup 54
Morning Forest Maple Granola 54
Vibrant Vegetable Tofu Scramble 55
Superfood Chia Seed Breakfast Bowl 55
Arkansas Apple Oatmeal 55
Silky Whole Wheat Strawberry Pancakes 56
Grown-Up Vegan Chocolate Milk 56
Quinoa Sensation Early Morning Porridge 57
No-Egg Pop Eye's Spinach Quiche..57
Carrotastic Apple Muffins 58
Vegan Variety Poppy Seed Scones 58
Vegan French Crepes..59
Homemade Raisin Rice Pudding 59
Spiced Holiday Cranberry Oatmeal 60
Spelt Flour Banana Muffins 60
Make-Your-Own vegan Muesli 61
Morning Glory Vegan Pumpkin Muffins 61
Savory Breakfast Indian Flatbread..61
Arabic Kidney Bean Breakfast 62
Date and Walnut Muffins 62
Blackberry Morning Smoothie 63
Vegan Tropical Pina Colada Smoothie 63
Enriching Oatmeal Strawberry Smoothie 64
Mango Chia Smoothie..64

Chapter 6: Lunch-Ready Vegan Wraps 65

Garbanzo Bean Naan Wrap 66
Mushroom Rice Noodle Wrap 66
Chinese-Inspired Vegan Wrap 66
Foodie Lover's Lettuce Wrap 67
Acing Avocado Rice Rolls 67
Lentil Tahini Lettuce Wraps 68
Black Bean and Sweet Potato Wrap 68
California-Based Hummus Wrap 69
Winter Garlic Spring Rolls 69
Curried Potato Wrap 70
Tofu and Spiced Nut Wrap 70
Soy Sauce and Mushroom Tofu Lettuce Wrap 71
Kale Cravings Wrap 71
Homemade Vegan Flour Tortillas 72
Homemade Vegan Corn Tortillas 72

Chapter 7: Vegan Soups, Chilis, and Stews 73

Burst Your Belly Vegan Tortilla Soup 74
Mediterranean Pasta Soup 74
Protein-Revving Lentil Vegetable Soup 75
Quizzical Quinoa Soup 75
Autumnal Apple and Squash Soup 76
Barley Country Living Soup 76
Spicy Vegetable Soup 77
"Cheese" Vegetable Soup 77
Red Quinoa and Black Bean Soup 78
October Potato Soup 79
Sunny Orange Carrot Soup 79
Lentil Luxury Soup 80
Broccoli Cheddar Vegan Soup 80
Curried Lentil Squash Stew 81
Vitamin C-Stocked Barley Soup 81
Apple and Carrot Ginger Soup 82
Indian-Inspired Spiced Broccoli Soup 82
Christmastime Calm Soup 83
Mushroom Quinoa Soup 83
Roasted Tomato and Onion Soup 84
Groovy Gazpacho Soup 84
Sweet Pie Strawberry Almond Soup 85
Super Vegetable Vegan Chili 85
Vegan Mexicano Chili 85
Beer Rejoice Vegan Chili 86
Vegan Sunny Potato Stew 86
Vegan Faux Chicken Noodle Soup 87

Vegan Faux Beef Stew..87
Sweet Potato Slow Cooker Chili...88
Extraordinary Slow Cooker Lentil Chili..88

Chapter 8: Tempting Tempeh Recipes Galore

Chapter 8: Tempting Tempeh Recipes Galore...89
Make-Your-Own Tempeh..90
Ultimate Seeded Tempeh Cutlets...90
Asian-Inspired Tempeh Satay..91
Warm Winter Night Tempeh Stew..91
Smoked Tempeh..92
Tempeh Mexican Tamale Pie...92
Tropical Pineapple Tempeh with Green Beans..93
Rambling Tempeh Reuben..94
Tempeh "Tuna" Salad..94
French Tempeh Ratatouille..94
Good Morning Tempeh Bacon..95
Fried Glory Garlic Tempeh..95
Marinated Snow Pea Tempeh...96
Make Your Own Chimichurri with Tempeh..96
Comfort Food Grilled Cheese with Tempeh...97
Tropical Coconut Tempeh with Kale..97
Cucumber with Tempeh Skewers..98
Hummus and Tempeh Sandwich...98
Chermoula Chipper Tempeh Munchers...99

Chapter 9: Sunny Seitan-Based Recipes

Chapter 9: Sunny Seitan-Based Recipes..101
Make Your Own Seitan...102
Super Seitan Fajitas...102
BBQ-Doused Seitan...103
Seitan Slow Cooked Chow Mein...103
Dee South Seitan Fried Chicken...104
Asian-Inspired Hoisin Sauce Stir Fry...104
Faux "Beef" Seitan Stew...105
Seitan Slow Cooker Rice Pilaf..105
Vietnamese Seitan Pho...105
Friday Afternoon Seitan "BLT" Sandwich...106
Indian-Inspired Curry Seitan Kebabs...106
Fresh Herbed Barley and Seitan Pilaf..107
Chicago Lover's Seitan Au Jus...107
Spicy Wild West Seitan Wings...108
New Orleans Sensation Seitan..108
Super Slow Cooked Seitan Tandoori...109
Norway's Seitan Stew..109
Dinner Date Coconut Breaded Seitan..110
Mapled Seitan Sandwich..110

Spiced Seitan Garlic Wrap 110

Asian-Inspired Sweet and Sour Seitan 111

Chicken-Flavored Seitan Tacos 111

Italian Seitan with Dip 112

Faux Canard BBQ Pizza 112

Broccoli with Seitan Marinated Kabobs 113

Chicago-Style Smoked Seitan Brisket 113

Inspired Chicken-Fried Seitan with Greens 114

Living the High Life Seitan Steaks 115

Warm Evening Seitan Beef Stew 115

Vibrant Colored Quinoa and Seitan Salad 116

Eggplant Agenda Seitan Stew 116

Seitan at the Summertime Deli Sandwich 117

Thanksgiving Dinner Seitan "Turkey" 117

Cilantro and Lime Seitan Munch 118

Taco Tuesday Spicy Seitan 118

Festival Occasion Teriyaki Seitan 119

Asian-Inspired Seitan Rolls 119

Vietnamese-Inspired Faux Duck Sandwich 120

Gotta Love It Seitan Piccada 120

Middle Eastern Seitan Shawarma 121

Seitan Alice Pineapple Rice 121

Ancient Orange Vegan Seitan 122

Seitan Mixed with Polenta 122

Coconut Spinach Seitan Sloppy Joes 123

Lemoned Seitan 123

Spiced Seitan Curry 124

Seitan Roulade Made with a Vegan Stuffing 124

Chapter 10: Tofu-Based Dinner Recipes

Chapter 10: Tofu-Based Dinner Recipes 125

Make-At-Home Tofu 126

Peanut Sauce Tofu Sandwiches 126

Tofu Tundra Scramble 127

Noodle Tofu Salad 127

Asparagus and Tofu Red Curry 128

BBQ Blast Off Tofu 128

Tropical Coconut Tofu Soup 129

Indian-style Curry Vindaloo with Tofu 129

Sizzlin' BBQ Tofu Burgers 130

Indian-Inspired Tofu Garam Masala 130

Italian Tofu Lasagna 131

Divine Tofu-Based Hummus 131

African-Inspired Tofu Dinner 132

Indian-Inspired Tofu Keema 132

Chinese Braised Tofu 133

Vegan Stroganoff 133
Samurai Tofu Salad 134
Cauliflower-Based Tofu Masala 134
Tofu "Meatloaf" 135
Tofu-Based Split Pea Soup 135

Chapter 11: Bean and Lentil Based Dinner Recipes 137

Flaxseed and Quinoa Crisp Gluten Cakes 138
Lentil-Based Taco Meat 138
Lentil Cranberry Meatballs 139
Chickpea Sweet Potato Burgers 139
Mean Green Chickpea Creation 140
Chinese Roasted Vegetable Bowl 140
Mapled Sweet Potato and Lentils 141
Layered Quick-Fix Bean Salad 141
Spiced Chickpea Burgers 142
Potato and Bean Salad 142
Stunning Rosemary Red Soup 143
Quinoa Creation Chili 143
Moscow Bean Salad 144
Faux Noodle Chickpea Salad 144
Mexicano and Chickpea Salad 144
Black Bean Revving Soup 145

Chapter 12: Vegan Pasta Recipes 147

Garlic and Tomato Penne Pasta 148
Faux Veggie Macaroni and Cheese 148
Bursting Vegan Stuffed Shells 149
Cauliflower-Based Fettuccini 149
Avocado-Based Pasta 150
Walnut-Based Pesto Pasta 150
Orange Butternut Squash Sage Linguine 151
Ginger-Based Coconut Linguine 151
Vegan Prepared Alfredo Sauce 152

Chapter 13: Roasted Vegetables and Other Delicious Vegan Sides 153

Green Beans with Grape Tomatoes 154
Super-Delicious Vegan Gravy 154
Thanksgiving Cranberry Sauce 154
Stunning Steamed Asparagus 155
Mapled Carrots with Dill Seasoning 155
Electric Garlic Kale 155
Lemony Snicket Garlic Broccoli 156
Super-Hot Red Cherry Tomatoes 156

Roasted Cauliflower 156
Super-Sweet Sweet Potato Casserole 157
Creamed Fall Corn 157
Zucchini Side Casserole 158
Southern Living Collard Greens 158
To the Side Roasted Butternut Squash 159
Super Summer Grilled Zucchini Flats 159
Beautiful Table Acorn Squash 159
Salty Squash Fries...160
Fried Green Zucchini 160
Glazed-Over Mustard Greens...161
Beans and Greens..161
Garlic-Based Spinach Side...161
Creamy Tofu Spinach 162
Lemoned Chard 162
Fall Time Side: Apples and Sweet Potatoes 163
Thyme for Maple Syrup Sweet Potato Fries 163
All Beet Up Sweet Potato 163
Super-Easy Applesauce 164
Currant is Current Applesauce..164
Primary Pear Applesauce 165
Craving Craisin Bulguar 165
South of the Border Mexican Quinoa...166
Garbanzo-Based Quinoa...166
Pesky Pesto Quinoa..166
Garlic Mashed Potatoes 167
Chived Vegan Sour Cream Mashed Potatoes 167
Sweet Mashed Carrots and Potatoes 167
Cheezin' Potato Faux Pancakes 168
Easy Microwavable Baked Potato 168
Cashewed Rice Pilaf 169
Broccoli and Rice Evening Casserole 169

Chapter 14: 50 Vegan Dessert Recipes 171

Autumnal Pumpkin Cookies 172
Trouble Chocolate-Chocolate Cookies...172
Oatmeal Cinnamon Bars...173
Vegan Vanilla Almond Cookies 173
Vegan Lover's Ginger Cookies...174
French Lover's Coconut Macaroons 174
Elementary Party Vegan Oatmeal Raisin Cookies 175
Classic Gluten-Free Cranberry Orange Muffin 175
Granola Grammar Muffins..176
Revving Apple Parsnip Muffin 176
Careful Carrot Muffin...177

Crunchy Peanut Butter Muffins with Ginger 178
Lemon Ginger Bread 178
Zucchini Chocolate Crisis Bread 179
Pull-Apart Vegan Monkey Bread..179
Vegan Pumpkin Bread 180
Banana Blueberry Bread..180
Creative Chocolate "Cream" Pie 181
Vegan Lemon Meringue Pie 182
Vegan Apple Cobbler Pie 182
Vegan Vanilla Ice Cream...183
Vibrant Lemon Millet Cookies 183
Vegan Strawberry Pie 184
Vegan Pumpkin and Chocolate Pie 184
Vegan Chocolate Cake...185
Very Blueberry Morning Coffee Cake...186
Good Morning Protein Pancakes 186
Vegan-Inspired Coconut Cake...187
Upside Down 3-Level Apple Nut Cake 187
Home Made Vegan Peppermint Patties 188
Groovy Christmas Time Peanut Butter Balls 189
Gluten-Free Chocolate Nubbins 189
MM-Good Chocolate Macarons 190
Faux Larabars with Chocolate Chips 190
Better than Heaven Almond Butter Cups 191
Easy Vegan Chocolate Frosting...191
No-Bake Rockin' Roll Bars 192
Everything Raw Vegan Chocolate Fudge 192
Chocolate Protein Balls 193
Coconut Craving Chocolate Bars 193
Smooth Vegan Tapioca Pudding Recipe 194
Avocado-Based Mousse...194

Chapter 15: Luscious Vegan Drink Recipes
....195
Chocolate Creation Hemp Smoothie..196
Non-Dairy Hot Chocolate..196
Vegan and Healthy Christmas Cocktail 196
Date with Cinnamon Smoothie..197
Natural Vegan Energy Slurp..197
Make Your Own Almond Milk 197
Make Your Own Oat Milk 198
Fall Time Pumpkin Pie Smoothie..198
Vegan Green Rough Rider Smoothie 199

Conclusion 201

Introduction

The switch to a healthier, better lifestyle can be a tricky one to make. After all: you hear constant voices telling you which ways to eat, which ways to exercise, and which ways to live—and many of these things are contradicting.

The truth of the matter is, people are eating too much meat, too much dairy, and too many animal products overall. Our disease rates are skyrocketing and our fat levels are rising by the day. How can you beat back against this world of animal fats and disease?

You must go vegan.

HEALTH BENEFITS OF GOING VEGAN:

Seriously. The health benefits are unrivaled. According to recent scientific studies, vegans live better, more consciously, and far healthier than anyone else. In fact, nearly every recipe in this e-book can be made from scratch at home. Begin to learn the steps to create your own vegan cheeses, your own vegan sour creams, your own tofu, your own seitan, and your own tempeh—from ingredients that are very easy to find in the world. By choosing the vegan lifestyle, you are choosing a lifestyle that encapsulates a preservative-free existence. You are looking away from packaged foods AND unhealthy meats and cheeses. And as a result, you are choosing health.

VEGAN AND NUTRITION:

As you know, vegan lifestyle incorporates many fruits and vegetables. It's pulsing with vitamin C, which works to enrich your gum health and beat back against free radicals that work to cause cancer in your cells.

Furthermore, vegetables like broccoli and Brussels sprouts are vibrant with phytochemicals, which work to eliminate bad free radicals, heal your body's unhealthy cells, eliminate dead cells, and boost your cells immune response.

VEGANISM FIGHTS DISEASE

It's clear that the vegan lifestyle fights back against diseases like cataracts, breast cancer, arthritis, cholesterol, cardiovascular disease, and osteoporosis. It further works to bring your body back to an appropriate body mass index and help you lose weight. Your skin will brighten; your body odor will decrease at an undeniable level (because of the lack of cholesterol and diary products).

TIPS FOR GOING VEGAN

How should you begin your vegan journey? Look toward a brighter future with the following tips and tricks for going vegan:

1. Don't Go to the Convenience Frozen Section.

Okay. So, as you start your vegan journey, it's essential you don't start by relying on frozen vegan products. Try to assimilate yourself into the natural foods, falling away from preservative-rich things like vegan burritos and frozen vegan pizzas.

2. Load Up on Vegetables.

When you go vegan, you're opening your mind to endless vegetable possibilities. Awesome! Head to the produce aisle at your grocery store, and dip into the interesting vegetable options. Beyond the chicken, steak, and turkey of your past life, each vegetable has so much to offer you.

3. Stay strong in your new lifestyle choice.

When you begin to understand how best to cook and LIVE vegan, you won't find this lifestyle so difficult. But you might, alas, find yourself a little lost in the first few days. Don't give up.

4. Hold strong in your beliefs.

Many people will ask you WHY you went vegan. Don't even give them an answer. Instead, hold your head up high and walk the vegan walk. This is your decision to get healthier and more fit. Don't give your decision to anyone else.

5. Pack vegan food on your travels.

Despite your veganism, the rest of the world hasn't caught up. Non-vegan foods run amok throughout the world, and It's best that you stay abreast of the situation with a few snacks of your own.

All things considered, this vegan lifestyle alters your life in every single way: from your hair follicles to the way you greet people in the morning—with a little extra energy. You can change your life; you can fuel yourself with wellness. During the next 365 days, choose one recipe per day to enhance your life. Find your favorites, and create your vegan diet lifestyle.

Remember the following things:

1. The vegan lifestyle yields essential benefits to your heart, your brain, your waistline, and your overall wellness.

2. The vegan lifestyle provides you with all the amino acids, nutrients, and vitamins your body requires to operate well.

3. Eliminating saturated fats from your diet can reduce your high blood pressure and help you avoid future bouts of illness.

4. You can avoid future struggles with colon cancer with your enhanced intake of fiber.

5. You can fuel yourself with necessary potassium, which helps to keep your cell balance in check and keep you free of toxins and diseases.

Chapter 1:
Appetizers:

Southwestern Style Mini Tortilla Pizzas

Recipe Makes 24 servings.

Ingredients:

6 6-inch corn tortillas
½ diced green pepper
½ diced red pepper
1 diced tomato
8 ounces green chilis

3 sliced scallions
¼ cup diced cilantro
1 ¾ cup nacho-style non-dairy cheese
(recipe found here)

Directions:

Begin by pre heating your oven to 400 degrees Fahrenheit.

Next, place each of the tortillas in one layer on two baking sheets. Place the ingredients overtop the corn tortillas, placing the non-dairy cheese overtop last.

Bake the tortillas for ten minutes. The cheese should begin to bubble. Slice the tortillas into four pieces, and serve them warm before a party. Enjoy!

Spinach Vegan Puff-Pastry Strudel

Recipe Makes 24 pieces.

Ingredients:

2 potatoes
8 ounces spinach
2 sheets Pedderidge Farm puff pastry
½ cup diced parsley

2 tbsp. minced dill
3 sliced scallions
½ cup sliced sun-dried tomatoes

Directions:

Begin by allowing the puff pastry to thaw for about an hour.

While this is happening, allow the potatoes to bake in either the microwave or in the oven at 400 degrees Fahrenheit. Make sure to plunge your fork into the potatoes to give them air holes. They usually cook in the oven for about forty minutes and in the microwave for about twenty. After they're cooked but still a bit hard to the touch, place them in cold water.

Next, preheat the oven to 400 degrees Fahrenheit—if you didn't already to bake the potatoes.

Afterwards, place the spinach, scallions, parsley, and dill together in a large skillet. Allow the leaves to wilt on medium heat. After about a minute, drain out the greens and remove moisture.

After the potatoes have cooled, peel them and slice them.

Position a pastry sheet on a baking sheet and fold it out from itself. Scatter out the potato slices over the puff pastry, and cover the pastry with all the greens and tomatoes.

Roll the pastry over itself to create the strudel-style, with an appropriate jelly-roll. Make sure to tuck in the ends in order to keep the filling inside. Slash at the top of the strudel in even intervals to create about twelve different pieces.

Repeat the above instructions with the rest of the ingredients and the second puff pastry.

Allow the puff pastries to bake for twenty minutes. Cool them until they're warm, and serve them.

Enjoy!

Vegan Green Quesadillas

Recipe Makes 6 Servings.

Ingredients:

6 8-inch flour tortillas
3 minced scallions

1 diced avocado
1 ¼ cup grated non-dairy cheese

Directions:

Begin by spreading both tortillas out on a flat surface and dividing the grated cheese, the avocado, and the scallions overtop one half of each of the tortillas.

Next, fold the tortillas evenly in half, and cook the quesadillas on a hot griddle. Make sure to flip the tortillas when the first side is golden. Flip them easily and carefully.

In order to serve the quesadillas, slice them to make easy-to-take wedges, and serve warm.

Easy Mean White Bean Dip

Recipe Makes 10 servings.

Ingredients:

3 minced garlic cloves
16 ounces white beans
1 tbsp. olive oil
1 tsp. chili powder
3 drops hot pepper sauce

2 tbsp. lemon juice
1 tsp. salt
½ tsp. cumin

Directions:

Begin by placing all the ingredients together in a food processor, and process them for about two minutes or until they're smooth. If your mixture is too thick and chunky, add water to the food processor until you reach your desired consistency. Enjoy!

Bean and Carrot Spirals

Recipe Makes 24 servings.

Ingredients:

4 8-inch flour tortillas
1 ½ cups of Easy Mean White Bean dip
(recipe found here)

10 ounces spinach leaves
½ cup diced carrots
½ cup diced red peppers

Directions:

Begin by preparing the bean dip, seen above. Next, spread out the bean dip on each tortillas, making sure to leave about a ¾ inch white border on the outside of the tortillas. Next, place spinach in the center of the tortilla, followed by carrots and red peppers. Roll the tortillas into tight rolls, and then cover each of the rolls with plastic wrap or aluminum foil. Allow them to chill in the fridge for twenty-four hours.

Afterwards, remove the wrap from the spirals and remove the very ends of the rolls. Slice the rolls into six individual spiral pieces, and arrange them on a platter for serving. Enjoy!

Asian-Inspired Summer Goi Cuan

Recipe Makes 24 rolls.

Ingredients:

24 round rice paper wrappers
6-7 cups of jasmine tea
2 de-ribbed and separated lettuce heads
9 ounces cooked thin rice vermicelli noodles
½ cup Thai basil leaves

1 ½ cups enoki mushrooms
1 cup chopped mint
¼ cup chopped cilantro
½ cup sliced scallions
2 sliced carrots
1 sliced cucumber

Directions:

Begin by preparing the tea and keeping it warm. Next, dip each of the rice paper wrappers into the tea. Place the rice wrappers on a cutting board, and place a layer of lettuce in the center. Enter in a bit of all of the above ingredients.

Next, fold over the bottom of the rice paper overtop of the filling. Tuck in the sides, and continue to wrap the rice up.

Do this for each of the 24 rice paper wrappers, and chill the rolls prior to serving. Enjoy!

Very Vegan Crunchy Chile Nachos

Recipe Makes 8 Servings.

Ingredients:

14 corn tortillas.
1 minced onion
2 tsp. olive oil
1 diced tomato
1 diced garlic

1 tbsp. white flour
2 diced jalapeno peppers
4 tbsp. rice milk
7 ounce grated non-dairy cheddar cheese

Directions:

Begin by preheating the oven to 375 degrees Fahrenheit.

Next, slice each of the corn tortillas into wedges and place them out on a baking sheet. Allow them to bake for twenty minutes. Afterwards, remove the chips and allow them to cool.

Heat garlic and onion together in some olive oil and sauté them for five minutes. Afterwards, add the tomatoes and the jalapenos, and continue to cook and stir for one minute. Add the rice milk.

Next, pour the non-dairy cheese into the mixture, and stir the ingredients together until the cheese completely melts. Remove the skillet form the heat.

Spread out the tortillas on a large plate, and pour the created cheese sauce overtop the chips. Serve warm.

Yummy Roasted Mushrooms

Recipe Makes 8 Servings.

Ingredients:

2 pounds cremini mushrooms
2 ½ tbsp. olive oil
spinach for serving

2 tbsp. soy sauce
2 minced garlic cloves

Directions:

Begin by preheating the oven to 350 degrees Fahrenheit.

Slice up the mushrooms, and place the mushrooms in a large mixing bowl with the rest of the ingredients—except for the spinach. Bake the ingredients in a baking dish for thirty minutes.

Next, remove the baked ingredients, and place them overtop of the spinach in a serving bowl. Enjoy.

Tofu Nuggets with Barbecue Glaze

Recipe Makes 9 Servings.

Ingredients:

32 ounces tofu
1 cup quick vegan barbecue sauce

Directions:

Begin by preheating the oven to 425 degrees Fahrenheit.

Next, slice the tofu and blot the tofu with clean towels. Next, slice and dice the tofu and completely eliminate the water from the tofu material.

Stir the tofu with the vegan barbecue sauce, and place the tofu on a baking sheet.

Bake the tofu for fifteen minutes. Afterwards, stir the tofu and bake the tofu for an additional ten minutes.

Enjoy!

Savory Scallion Pancakes

Recipe Makes 24 mini pancakes.

Ingredients:

1 cup spelt flour
1 cup and 2 tbsp. rice milk
1 cup sliced scallions

1 tsp. salt
olive oil for cooking

Directions:

Begin by combining the above ingredients in a mixing bowl. Stir the ingredients well until they're smooth.

Afterwards, oil up a griddle and place about 1/8 of a cup of batter on the griddle for each pancake. Cook each side of the pancake to achieve a golden brown color.

Next, place the pancakes on a plate, and cover the pancakes while you continue to cook the rest of the batter. Place the pancakes out on a nice platter, and serve warm.

Broiled Japanese Eggplants

Recipe Makes 4 Servings.

Ingredients:

2 tbsp. white wine
2 tbps. Sweet rice wine
3 tbsp. agave netar

4 tbsp. mellow white miso
4 Japanese eggplants, sliced in half, de-stemmed

Directions:

Begin by simmering the sweet rice wine and the white wine together in a saucepan. Simmer them together for two minutes. Afterwards, add the miso and stir the ingredients until they're smooth. Add the agave nectar. At this time, reduce the stovetop heat to low. Continue to heat this mixture while you initiate the next step.

Next, place the eggplants with their cut-sides down onto the baking sheet. Place the baking sheet in the broiler for three minutes. Make sure that they do not burn. After three minutes, flip them and cook them for an additional three minutes. The tops should be brown.

After the eggplants have cooked, layer the created sauce overtop of them. Place them in the broiler for about forty-five seconds. Afterwards, remove the eggplants and serve them warm. Enjoy!

Smokin' Peanut and Tofu

Recipe Makes 10 servings.

Ingredients:

7 ounces smoked tofu
6 celery stalks
2 ounces roasted peanuts

3 tbsp. chili oil
½ tsp. sugar
salt to taste

Directions:

Begin by slicing the tofu into small cubes and squeezing them of their water. Afterwards, slice up the celery into small strips the same size as the small tofu squares.

Allow water to boil in a small saucepan. Add the celery and allow it to blanch for one minute. Afterwards, remove the celery and allow it to cool. Shake it dry.

Bring all the above ingredients together in a bowl for an essential appetizer. Enjoy!

Groovy Indian Samosas

Recipe Makes 4 Servings.

Ingredients:

¼ cup olive oil

2 diced onions

1 tsp. mustard seeds
½ tsp. salt
3 tsp. curry powder
1 diced carrot
2 diced potatoes

1 cup diced green beans
1 cup frozen peas
1/3 cup water
8 ounces phyllo pastry
sunflower or olive oil for frying

Directions:

Begin by warming up the olive oil in a skillet, and adding the mustard seeds, allowing them to heat until they pop. Add the onions, and cook them for five minutes.

Next, pour in the curry powder and the salt. Fry these together for one and a half minutes. Next, add the carrots, the potatoes, the peas, the beans, and the water. Cook this mixture together for fifteen minutes on LOW. The vegetables should be soft.

Next, slice up the phyllo pastry to create long strips. Take one strip and place a tbsp.. of the created filling in the strip, at the end. Fold this strip diagonally to create a triangle. Continue this folding until the very end of the strip. Afterwards, seal up the end with water.

Repeat the above steps with all the remaining phyllo strips.

Afterwards, half-fill a wok with sunflower oil. Heat the oil to 350 degrees Fahrenheit. Next, fry up the samosas for three minutes until they reach a golden color. Allow them to drain, and then serve them warm. Enjoy!

Artichoke Attack Appetizer

Recipe Makes 6 Servings.

Ingredients:

10 ounces asparagus
8 ounces button mushrooms
8 ounces artichoke hearts
1 chopped dill pickle
1 sliced zucchini

¼ cup chopped parsley
½ cup vegan mayonnaise (recipe here)
1 juiced lemon
salt and pepper to taste

Directions:

Begin by slicing up the mushrooms and placing them in a skillet with about ¼ cup water. Cover the skillet and allow them to steam on medium-heat for two and a half minutes. Next, drain the mushrooms and allow them to cool.

To the side, trim at the bottom of the asparagus, and slice the asparagus into smaller, one-inch pieces. Place the asparagus in the mushroom skillet, and place just about three tbsp.. of water at the bottom. Steam the asparagus until the asparagus is a bright green. Drain the asparagus, and rinse it.

Bring the mushrooms and asparagus together in a serving bowl. Bring in the artichoke hearts, the dill pickle, the zucchini, the parsley, the mayonnaise, the lemon, and the salt and pepper, Mix well, and enjoy.

Vegan Creation Coleslaw

Recipe Makes 3 cups.

Ingredients:

1 cup cashews
2 tbsp. agave syrup
juice of 2 lemons
1 tsp. mustard
1 tsp. Dijon mustard

1/3 cup sliced almonds
1/3 cup shredded cabbage
3 cups shredded spinach
4 springs parsley

Directions:

Begin by adding cashews, agave, and lemon juice together in a food processor. Process well, and add the mustards.

Next, mix together the almonds, the spinach, the cabbage, and the parsley. Add the sauce to the mixture, and serve. Enjoy!

Lucky Lemon Mushrooms

Recipe Makes 6 Servings.

Ingredients:

1 tsp. agave nectar
3 tbsp. lemon juice
1 tbsp. olive oil

2 minced garlic cloves
10 ounces sliced portabella mushrooms

Directions:

Bring together the agave nectar, the lemon juice, the olive oil, and the minced garlic in a mixing bowl. Place the sliced mushrooms in the created mixture, and stir them together. Next, place the mushrooms in a baking pan, and pour the marinade overtop of them.

Broil the mushrooms for four minutes. After four minutes, stir the mushrooms. Broil them for an additional five minutes. The mushrooms should be darker. Remove the mushrooms, and serve them warm. Enjoy!

Finger-Licking Appetizer Pretzels

Recipe Makes 5 cups.

Ingredients:

3 cups small pretzels
3 tbsp. soy sauce
1 tsp. cinnamon

3 tbsp. agave nectar
2 cups unsalted peanuts or almonds
½ tsp. ginger

Directions:

Begin by preheating the oven to 300 degrees Fahrenheit. Next, bring together the soy sauce, the cinnamon, the agave nectar, and the ginger in a medium-sized bowl. Stir well. Add the pretzels and the nuts and continue to stir.

Spread this creation over a baking sheet, and bake them for twenty minutes. You should stir them every five minutes.

Next, allow the pretzels to cool, and set them out as a party appetizer.

Enjoy!

No-Egg Deviled Tomatoes

Recipe Makes 16 Servings.

Ingredients:

16 ounces garbanzo beans
2 tbsp. nutritional yeast
½ cup vegan mayonnaise
2 tsp. mustard

1 ½ tbsp. lemon juice
1 tsp. curry powder
salt and pepper to taste
10 Roma tomatoes

Directions:

Bring together the mustard, the lemon juice, the yeast, the mayonnaise, the garbanzos, the salt, and the pepper together in a food processor. Pulse the mixture together.

Next, slice the tomatoes into equal halves. Remove the pulp of the tomatoes. Next, stuff each of the tomatoes with the created mixture, and arrange the no-egg deviled tomatoes on a platter.

Enjoy!

Quick-Fix Cashew and Date

Recipe Makes 24 Servings.

Ingredients:

2 tbsp. shredded coconut
12 dates
12 roasted cashews

1/3 cup cashew butter

Directions:

Begin by slicing the dates in half and taking out the seeds. Portion the cashew butter into the dates, and split each of the cashews in half. Place one half of each cashew in one half of each date, and arrange the dates on a nice plate. Enjoy!

No-Meat Pre-Dinner Meatballs

Recipe Makes 12 meatballs.

Ingredients:

1 diced onion
1 cup diced mushrooms
1 ½ tbsp. olive oil
2 tbsp. tomato paste
2 diced garlic cloves
1 cup diced walnuts
2 tbsp. wheat germ

1/3 cup chopped parsley
3 tbsp. oats
2 tsp. tamari
1 tsp. paprika
½ tsp. thyme
½ tsp. onion powder
1 tbsp. nutritional yeast

Directions:

Begin by preheating the oven to 375 degrees Fahrenheit.

Next, place the olive oil in a frying pan and sauté the garlic, the onions, and the mushrooms for about five minutes. Place these ingredients in a food processor, and add all of the other ingredients to the food processor, as well. Blend all the ingredients until they're completely smooth.

Next, formulate the blended ingredients into small balls, and place them on a baking sheet. Cover the baking sheet, and bake the meatballs for thirty minutes. Afterwards, flip over the meatballs and cook them for an additional ten minutes without a cover. Allow them to cool, and enjoy.

Autumnal Roasted Chestnuts

Recipe Makes 8 Servings.

Ingredients:

1 ½ pounds chestnuts with shells

Directions:

Begin by slitting the shells of each of the chestnuts utilizing a sharp paring knife. Pierce the shell clear through to the chestnut.

Next, place the chestnuts in a popcorn popper or large skillet and allow it to heat over a flame. Continue to shake the skillet to heat all sides of the chestnuts.

Do this cooking technique for fifteen minutes. After the chestnuts shells are black, place the nuts to the side and wait until they're cooled before peeling and munching on them warm.

Enjoy!

Indian Garbanzo Beans

Recipe Makes 6 Servings.

Ingredients:

2 tbsp. agave nectar
1 ½ tbsp. soy sauce
1 tsp. white wine vinegar

16 ounces chickpeas
1 tsp. paprika

Directions:

Begin by stirring together the agave nectar, the soy sauce, and the vinegar together in a small bowl. Add the chickpeas. Pour this mixture into a saucepan, and allow the ingredients to simmer on medium heat for about eight minutes.

Toss the paprika over the garbanzo beans, and stir in order to properly season the garbanzo beans. Serve as an appetizer, and enjoy!

Finger-Licking' Spiced Crackers

Recipe Makes 60 crackers.

Ingredients:

1 tsp. xanthan gum
2 cups chickpea flour
½ cup sorghum flour
½ cup nutritional yeast
1/3 cup potato starch
2 tsp. salt
1 tsp. cumin
½ cup fresh diced cilantro

2 tsp. chili pepper powder
1 tsp. curry powder
½ tsp. coriander
½ cup olive oil
¼ tsp. methi powder
1 cup water

Directions:

Begin by preheating your oven to 350 degrees Fahrenheit.

Next, combine together the chickpea flour, the sorghum flour, the nutritional yeast, the potato starch, all the spices, and the salt. Stir well, and add the olive oil. Next, add the water, and begin to work with the dough with your hands. It should become sticky.

Next, add the cilantro, and continue to fold the dough in order to assimilate the herbs.

Roll out the dough on a floured counter space, and cut out the crackers utilize a cookie cuter.

Place the crackers on a baking sheet, and bake the crackers for thirty-five minutes. Allow them to cool, and enjoy!

Tempeh Finger Fries

Recipe Makes 4 Servings.

Ingredients:

8 ounces fry-sliced tempeh
1 tbsp. olive oil

2 tbsp. soy sauce
1 tsp. chili powder

Directions:

Begin by heating up the soy sauce and the olive oil together in a skillet for about two minutes. Afterwards, add the sliced tempeh, making sure to coat the tempeh with the sauce. Add the chili powder and stir well. Sauté this mixture well for about seven or eight minutes. The tempeh should be crisp on all sides.

Enjoy with your favorite dip!

Everyday Cantankerous Kale Chips

Recipe Makes 6 Servings.

Ingredients:

12 ounces kale
1 tbsp. olive oil
salt to taste

Directions:

Begin by de-stemming the kale and tearing the kale into chip-like pieces.

Rinse these leaves, and allow them to dry completely. After they've dried, preheat the oven to 325 degrees Fahrenheit.

Next, place the kale in a mixing bowl, and drizzle about a tbsp. of olive oil overtop of them. Mix up the kale to coat it with the oil. Place the kale leaves out on a baking sheet in one layer, and bake the kale chips for twenty minutes. After you remove the kale leaves, salt them and enjoy!

Freedom Sweet Fries

Recipe Makes 4 Servings.

Ingredients:

2 sliced sweet potato fries
1 tsp. paprika
2 tsp. olive oil

½ tsp. cumin
1 tsp. salt

Directions:

Begin by preheating the oven to 350 degrees Fahrenheit.

Next, stir together the sweet potatoes and all of the above ingredients in a large mixing bowl. Make sure to completely coat the sweet potato fries. Next, spread the sweet potato fries out on a baking sheet, and allow them to bake for fifty minutes. Serve warm, and enjoy

Baby Finger Burgers

Recipe Makes 4 Servings.

Ingredients:

15 ounce can of green lentils
2 tsp. paprika
½ tsp. garlic powder
¼ tsp. pepper
1 tbsp. tamari
1/3 cup wheat gluten

1 tsp. Worcestershire sauce
2 tbsp. olive oil
8 mini vegan buns
2 sliced dill pickles
8 toothpicks for skewering

Directions:

Begin by stirring together the paprika, the lentils, the garlic powder, the tamari, the pepper, and the Worcestershire sauce in a medium-sized bowl. Mash up the ingredients to make sure that most of the lentils are mashed.

Next, stir in the wheat gluten and continue to smash. You should create a dough ball. Remove about a tbsp. of the prepared dough, and place this dough on a clean surface. Lay out all sixteen balls of dough and flatten each of the balls into a hamburger patty.

Heat the olive oil in a skillet and place each patty in the skillet, frying each side for about five minutes.

Assemble your tiny burgers by placing the burger in the buns and administering your favorite toppings. (I chose dill pickles.) When you're finished, skewer the hamburgers and serve them warm at your party. Enjoy!

Mediterranean Garbanzo-Bean Fritters

Recipe Makes 4 Servings.

Ingredients:

1 cup garbanzo bean flour
1 tsp. salt
½ tsp. cumin
1 ¼ cup chopped spinach
¼ tsp. baking soda

4 minced garlic cloves
2 sliced scallions
1 cup drained garbanzo beans
1 cup olive oil

Directions:

Begin by preheating the oven to 200 degrees Fahrenheit.

Next, stir together the flour, salt, and cumin. Add hot water a little bit at a time in order to create a paste-like texture: like pancake batter. Allow this mixture to stand at room temperature for one hour.

Afterwards, add the baking soda, the garlic, and the spinach to the mixture. Stir. Next, add the scallions and the chickpeas.

Pour the olive oil in the skillet, and place the heat on medium. When you've heated the oil sufficiently, place the fritters on the oil and brown them for three minutes on each side. Drain the fritters on paper towels, and serve them with your favorite dipping sauce.

Super Rad-ish Avocado Salad

Recipe Makes 2 Salads.

Ingredients:

6 shredded carrots
6 ounces diced radishes

1 diced avocado
1/3 cup ponzu

Directions:

Bring all the above ingredients together in a serving bowl and toss. Enjoy!

Beauty School Ginger Cucumbers

Recipe Makes 14 slices.

Ingredients:

1 sliced cucumber
3 tsp. rice wine vinegar

1 ½ tbsp. sugar
1 tsp. minced ginger

Directions:

Bring all of the above ingredients together in a mixing bowl, and toss the ingredients well. Enjoy!

Chapter 2:
Dipping Sauces and Spreads

Romesco Sauce

Recipe Makes 2 cups

Ingredients:

4 tbsp. olive oil
¾ cup sliced almonds
3 inches of a baguette, sliced into smaller pieces
3 minced garlic cloves

2 ½ peeled and roasted red peppers
3 tsp. paprika
2 tbsp. diced parsley
3 tbsp. sherry vinegar
1 tsp. salt

Directions:

Begin by heating the olive oil in a skillet over medium. Add the almonds, the garlic, and the pieces of bread to the oil, and cook them for about five minutes.

Afterwards, place the bread, almonds, garlic, peppers, paprika, and parsley in the food processor. Create a paste. Lastly, add the vinegar and the salt. If you want to create a thinner consistency, add a bit more water or a bit more oil to your desired texture.

Enjoy!

Sun-Dried Tomato with Black Olive Flair Spread

Recipe Makes 2 cups.

Ingredients:

20 sun-dried tomatoes
2 diced onions
¾ cup water
1 ½ tbsp.. olive oil

2 diced garlic cloves
2 cups black olives
1 tsp. salt

Directions:

Begin by placing the sun-dried tomatoes in the water for over an hour in order to soften them.

During this time, place the olive oil in a skillet, and sauté up the onions, the garlic, and the salt. Sauté the ingredients for about ten minutes.

After the tomatoes are finished soaking, drain them and place them with the onions and the black olives. Place these ingredients in the food processor, and pulse the ingredients to make a chopped spread.

Enjoy over crackers!

Summertime Garlic Bean Dip

Recipe Makes 2 cups.

Ingredients:

2 sliced scallions
16 ounce can of navy beans
juice from one lemon

1/3 cup walnuts
½ tsp. salt

Directions:

Begin by bringing all the above ingredients together in a food processor. Puree the ingredients until you've reached your desired consistency. Adjust your seasonings as needed, and enjoy!

Spicy Lovin' Bean Dip

Recipe Makes 6 Servings.

Ingredients:

1 cup spicy refried beans (remember that these cans are usually vegan. Make sure to check your particular brand.)

2 sliced scallions
1 cup salsa
1 cup grated vegan cheese

Directions:

Begin by bringing the refried beans and the salsa together in a saucepan. Heat the mixture until it begins to bubble.

Afterwards, place half of this mixture in a medium-sized serving bowl. Sprinkle the scallions and half of the grated cheese in this in-between, and coat it with the rest of the beans. Sprinkle over the remaining vegan cheese, and keep the bean dip warm before you serve it. Enjoy!

Natural-Variety Cilantro Black Bean Dip

Recipe Makes 3 cups.

Ingredients:

2 cups canned black beans
½ cup chopped cilantro leaves
½ cup sliced scallions
1 ½ cups salsa
1 tsp. cayenne

1 tsp. salt

Directions:

Begin by placing all of the above ingredients together in a food processor. Blend the ingredients, and taste the dip in order to alter the seasonings, as you desire. Place the dip in a serving bowl, and enjoy with vegetables or tortilla chips!

Sun-Dried Sunny Tomato Tofu Dip

Recipe Makes 2 cups.

Ingredients:

1 diced onion
1 tbsp. olive oil
3 minced garlic cloves
1 package firm tofu
juice from 1 lemon

1/3 cup sun-dried tomato
¼ cup parsley leaves
1 tsp. cumin
½ tsp. thyme
salt and pepper to taste

Directions:

Begin by heating up the olive oil in a skillet over medium-high heat. Next, add the onion and sauté it until it's clear. Next, add the garlic and sauté for an additional three minutes.

Bring the onion and garlic together with the above listed ingredients in a food processor. Process the ingredients until you've reached your desired consistency. You can add water to make it looser.

Enjoy your tofu dip with vegetables or vegan crackers!

Turkish-Based Beet Muhummara Spread

Recipe Makes 4 cups.

Ingredients:

3 peeled and sliced fresh beets
½ cup Panko bead crumbs
1 ½ cups diced walnuts
1 tbsp. cumin

4 minced garlic cloves
2 tsp. salt
4 tbsp. olive oil
2 tbsp. molasses

Directions:

Bring all the above ingredients together in a food processor, adding olive oil as you please to reach your desired consistency. Enjoy with crackers or vegetables.

Green Pistachio Pesto

Recipe Makes 10 servings.

Ingredients:

1 cup arugula
1 ½ cups basil
1/3 cup olive oil
1/3 cup pistachio nuts (no shells)

3 tbsp. lemon juice
1 tsp. salt
1 ½ tsp. lemon zest

Directions:

Bring all the above ingredients together in a food processor, and process the ingredients until they're completely mixed. Enjoy.

Parsley Pea Pesto

Recipe Makes 1 ½ cups.

Ingredients:

1 cup parsley leaves
1 cup frozen peas
½ tsp. dried dill
juice from 1 lemon

1 cup no-shell pistachios
1/3 cup water
salt and pepper to taste

Directions:

Begin by cooking up the peas in a saucepan with a it of water.

After the peas are cooked, place all the ingredients together in a food processor until the mixture is completely pureed.

Afterwards, taste the pesto and add any other seasonings you might like. Enjoy!

Tofu Spinach Dip

Recipe Makes 2 cups.

Ingredients:

1 packaged silken tofu
½ cup diced cucumber
6 ounces spinach
1 diced scallion

1 tsp. dry dill
2 tsp. cumin
salt and pepper to taste

Directions:

Begin by placing the cucumber out on a paper towel and allowing the cucumber to drain completely.

To the side, place the spinach, the tofu, the scallions, the dill, the cumin, and some salt and pepper into the food processor. Puree the ingredients.

Transfer this pureed mixture to a food processor, and add the cucumber. Stir well. Serve the mixture chilled. Enjoy!

Potatoes with Almond-Based Pesto

Recipe Makes 6 Servings.

Ingredients:

22 small potatoes
1/3 cup toasted almonds
1 cup parsley leaves
2 tbsp. olive oil

juice from 1 lemon
2 minced garlic cloves
salt and pepper to taste

Directions:

Begin by steaming up the potatoes until they're tender but retain their firmness. Allow them to cool. Then, cut them in half.

Bring all the other ingredients together in a food processor, and created a blended, textured pesto. Toss the halved potatoes together with the pesto, and serve the pesto potatoes warm. Enjoy!

Faux Chopped Liver

Recipe Makes 2 ¼ cups.

Ingredients:

2 tbsp. olive oil
1 cup toasted cashews
2 diced onions

1 cup thawed green beans
2 tbsp. lemon juice
salt and pepper to taste

Directions:

Begin by heating up the oil in a skillet. Allow the diced onions to cook over medium heat until they turn golden brown.

Afterwards, combine all the above ingredients together in a food processor. Puree the ingredients until you've reached your desired texture, and enjoy with crackers or vegetables.

Greek Tofu Tahini Dip

Recipe Makes 2 cups.

Ingredients:

1/3 cup sesame paste

1 package silken tofu

juice from 1 lemon
1/3 cup chopped dill
2 tbsp. nutritional yeast

1/3 cup white miso
1 diced scallion
pepper to taste

Directions:

Bring all the above ingredients together in a food processor. Process the ingredients until they're completely smooth. Transfer the above ingredients to a serving dish, and enjoy!

Eggplant and Tahini Mediterranean Spread

Recipe Makes 10 Servings.

Ingredients:

2 pounds eggplants
2 tbsp. olive oil
4 minced garlic cloves
1 diced onion

juice from 1 lemon
½ tsp. cumin
salt and pepper to taste

Directions:

Begin by preheating the oven to 450 degrees Fahrenheit.

Next, place the eggplants on a baking sheet, and place the eggplants beneath the broiler. The skin should be blackened and the eggplants should fall into themselves after about thirty-five minutes. Remove the vegetables and allow them to cool before removing the stems and the skin.

Next, heat up the oil in a skillet. Place the onions in the skillet and cook them until they're clear. Next, add the garlic, and sauté them for an additional three minutes.

Place the onion, the garlic, and the eggplant together in the food processor. Add the lemon, the cumin, and the salt and pepper, and process the mixture until it's completely pureed. Enjoy with crackers.

Tangy Artichoke-Based Roasted Eggplant Dip

Recipe Makes 6 Servings.

Ingredients:

1 pound eggplant
1 sliced celery stalk
12 ounce can of artichoke hearts
1/3 cup minced cilantro
1 sliced red pepper
2 tbsp. olive oil

1/3 cup sliced black olives
2 tbsp. red wine vinegar
salt and pepper to taste

Directions:

Begin by preheating the oven to 425 degrees Fahrenheit.

Next, place the eggplant on a baking sheet, and bake it for forty minutes. Remove the eggplant and allow it to cool. When it has cooled, remove the peel and dice up the insides of the eggplant. Place the eggplant pulp in a serving bowl along with the artichoke hearts and the other ingredients. Toss the ingredients well, and serve.

Chermoula Dipping Sauce

Recipe Makes 2 cups.

Ingredients:

2 tsp. cumin seeds
3 tbsp. olive oil
1 diced onion
4 minced garlic cloves
½ tsp. paprika
3 tbsp. lemon juice
2 tbsp. water

1 tbsp. orange juice
1 tsp. minced chili
¼ tsp. cayenne
½ tsp. saffron
2 cups minced cilantro
1 cup minced parsley

Directions:

Begin by heating the olive oil in a skillet and cooking the onion for seven minutes.

Next, sauté the cayenne, the cumin, the garlic, and the salt and pepper with the onions. Allow this mixture to cool.

Next, add the orange juice, the lemon juice, the water, the chili, and the saffron.

Add the cilantro and the parsley, last, and utilize as a dip or as a marinade. Enjoy!

Ultimate Vegan Hummus

Recipe Makes 8 Servings.

Ingredients:

20 ounce can of chickpeas
1/3 cup sesame paste
½ cup water
2 minced garlic cloves
juice from 1 lemon
1 tsp. cumin
salt and pepper to taste

Directions:

Begin by bringing all the above ingredients together in a food processor. Process the ingredients until you've reached your desired consistency. Enjoy with vegetables or crackers!

Summertime Tomato Guacamole

Recipe Makes 8 Servings.

Ingredients:

1 avocado
3 diced tomatoes
juice from 1 lemon
2 diced hot chilies

2 sliced scallions
1 tsp. cumin
1/3 cup diced cilantro leaves

Directions:

Slice and dice the tomatoes and the inside of the avocado. Bring all the above ingredients together in a food processor, and pulse the ingredients until they're just chopped. Make sure to leave them with a chunky consistency. Serve immediately, and enjoy.

Mean Bean Salsa

Recipe Makes 2 cups.

Ingredients:

1 cup drained black beans
1 cup diced tomatoes
1 cup canned corn
1 diced onion
juice from 1 lime

½ cup diced green pepper
2 diced hot chili peppers
1/3 cup chopped cilantro
½ tsp. cumin

Directions:

Bring all the ingredients together in a serving bowl and stir well. Chill the ingredients in the refrigerator, covered, for about three hours to allow the ingredient flavors to assimilate well. Enjoy!

Tropical Pineapple Chunky Salsa

Recipe Makes 1 ½ cups.

Ingredients:

1 cup diced pineapple

1/3 cup diced red peppers

1 chopped tomato
2 minced hot chili peppers
2 tbsp. lemon juice

2 sliced scallions
1/3 cup minced cilantro

Directions:

Bring all the above ingredients together in a serving bowl, and stir them well. Cover the ingredients and allow them to chill together in the refrigerator for about three hours. Enjoy with tortilla chips.

Vegetable-Based Guacamole

Recipe Makes 8 Servings.

Ingredients:

1 green pepper
3 tomatoes
juice from 1 lemon
2 avocadoes

2 minced garlic cloves
½ tsp. cumin
3 tbsp. minced cilantro
salt and pepper to taste

Directions:

Begin by roasting the green pepper and the tomato together in a broiler for about five minutes. The skins should become blackened. Allow them to cool in a paper bag.

Next, mash up the avocadoes in a medium-sized mixing bowl. Add the lemon juice, the garlic cloves, the cumin, and the cilantro.

Next, remove the skins from the green pepper and the tomato and slice and dice them. Position them in the avocado bowl, and stir well. Serve with tortilla chips, and enjoy.

Super Spicy Green Salsa

Recipe Makes 2 cups.

Ingredients:

1 diced onion
1 tbsp. olive oil
3 minced garlic cloves
2 diced jalapeno peppers
¾ pound husked tomatillos

1/3 cup chopped cilantro leaves
3 chopped scallions
juice from 1 lime
¼ tsp. salt

Directions:

Begin by heating the tablespoon of olive oil in a skillet. Add the garlic and the onion and sauté for about seven minutes.

Afterwards, position these ingredients in a food processor with all the other listed ingredients. Puree the ingredients, and then place them back in the saucepan. Allow the mixture to simmer for fifteen minutes over medium heat. Allow the mixture to cool, and then chill the mixture in the refrigerator prior to serving. Enjoy.

El Avocado Mambo Mango Salsa

Recipe Makes 2 cups.

Ingredients:

1 avocado
1 mango
1 diced onion
1 diced tomato

1 minced jalapeno
½ tsp. pepper
1 tsp. olive oil

Directions:

Begin by slicing and dicing the inside of the avocado. Peel the mango and slice and dice the inside. Prepare the rest of the ingredients, and position all the ingredients together in a serving bowl. Add the pepper and the oil, and toss the ingredients well.

Serve the salsa for your next appetizer, and enjoy!

Tomatillo and Yellow Corn Dip

Recipe Makes 2 cups.

Ingredients:

7 husked and quartered tomatillos
2 grilled ears of corn
1 diced red pepper
½ cup cilantro
2 chopped chilies

½ diced onion
1 tsp. cumin
juice from 1 lime
salt to taste

Directions:

Begin by cooking the ears of corn either on a skillet or on a grill. After they've cooled, slice off the kernels.

Mix the kernels and all of the other listed ingredients together in a food processor. Pulse the ingredients until it formulates a chopped mixture. Make sure not to puree.

Serve the ingredients in a serving dish, and enjoy!

Chapter 3:
Vegan Cheese Recipes

Good Gouda Vegan Cheese

Recipe Makes 3 cups of cheese.

Ingredients:

2 cups water
1/3 cup nutritional yeast flakes
½ cup diced carrots
2 tbsp. agar powder
½ cup diced cashews
3 tbsp. lemon juice
4 tbsp. sesame tahini

1 tsp. salt
2 tsp. onion powder
2 tbsp. Dijon mustard
½ tsp. dry mustard
½ tsp. turmeric
¼ tsp. cumin

Directions:

Begin by oiling the bottom of a bowl and setting it to the side.

Next, mix together the carrots and the water over medium-high heat. When it begins to boil, place the heat to low, and cover it. Cook the carrots for fifteen minutes. Afterwards, add the agar powder. Allow the mixture to boil once more. When it begins to boil, decrease the heat once more and allow it to simmer for twelve minutes.

Afterwards, add this mixture to a food processor or blender with the other ingredients. Process the mixture until it's completely smooth.

Pour this created mixture into a container, and cool the mixture without a cover in the fridge for about two hours. After two hours, cover the mixture and refrigerate it for twelve hours. The faux cheese and ready to serve! Enjoy.

What a Breeze Vegan Brie Cheese

Recipe Makes 2 ½ cups of cheese.

Ingredients:

1 ½ cups water
2 tbsp. wheat germ
½ cup diced cashews
3 tbsp. agar flakes
¼ cup nutritional yeast flakes
½ cup crumbled firm tofu

1/3 cup lemon juice
2 tsp. onion powder
2 tbsp. sesame tahini
1 tsp. salt
¼ tsp. ground coriander

Directions:

Begin by oiling the bottom of a pie plate and dusting the bottom of it with the wheat germ. Set this to the side.

Next, mix together the agar and the water in a saucepan over medium-high heat. When it begins to boil, decrease the heat to low and allow it to simmer for twelve minutes. Position this mixture to a blender and administer the remaining ingredients, as well. Puree the ingredients until they're completely mixed and smooth.

Pour this mixture over the wheat germ in the pie plate, and place the pie plate in the refrigerator. When it's cooled—uncovered—for two hours, cover the cheese and allow it to cool for twelve hours before serving. Enjoy.

"Cheddar Cheese" Vegan Spread

Recipe Makes 1 ½ cups.

Ingredients:

2 cups diced cashews
2 cups water
1 tbsp. tahini
1 tbsp. sun-dried tomatoes

½ tsp. liquid aminos
2 tsp. lemon juice
½ tsp. garlic powder
½ tsp. paprika

Directions:

Begin by mixing together the tomatoes, the cashews, and one and a half cups of water together in a medium-sized bowl. All the ingredients to soak together for two hours. After two hours, drain the ingredients and toss out the water.

Place this mixture in the food processor. Administer the rest of the ingredients, and puree them all together for a few minutes until you reach your smooth consistency. You can serve immediately. Enjoy!

Herb is the Word Vegan Cheese

Recipe Makes 2 cups.

Ingredients:

1 tsp. lemon juice
1 ¾ cup cashews
½ tsp. sea salt
1 tbsp. nutritional yeast

½ tsp. probiotic powder
1 tsp. basil
½ tsp. paprika
1 cup of water

Directions:

Begin by blending all of the ingredients together in a blender or food processor until you reach a smooth consistency. Note that you can add more water to reach a better, more-spreadable cheese.

Next, position a strainer over a medium-sized bowl, and place a cheesecloth inside. Pour the cheese mix into the strainer over the cheesecloth, and place another cheesecloth overtop. Bring the cheesecloths together to completely cover the cheese mix, and allow it to culture together at room temperature for twenty-four hours.

Next, position the cheese in a covered container and chill it in the refrigerator. Enjoy!

Pesto Tofu Cheese Spread

Recipe Makes 2 cups.

Ingredients:

1 pound firm tofu
4 tbsp. soy milk
½ cup pine nuts
3 tsp. lemon juice

3 tbsp. nutritional yeast flakes
1 tsp. salt
1 ½ tsp. red miso

Directions:

Bring all of the above ingredients together in a food processor, and blend the ingredients until you reach a creamy consistency. Serve the cheese either immediately or after you've chilled it. Enjoy!

Texas Smoked Cheddar Cheese

Recipe Makes 10 Servings.

Ingredients:

1 cup rice milk
1 cup cashews
½ cup carrots
1/3 cup vegan cream cheese
1/3 cup agar flakes
3 tbsp. lemon juice

1/3 cup nutritional yeast flakes
2 tsp. smoked paprika
1 tsp. salt
1 tsp. sweet paprika
½ tsp. turmeric

Directions:

Bring the carrots, the rice milk, and the cashews together in a saucepan, and heat the ingredients together over medium heat for eight minutes. The carrots should be crips. Add the agar flakes at this time, and keep the simmer humming for five minutes.

Next, position this mixture in a food processor with all of the other ingredients listed above. Process the ingredients to create a creamy texture.

Place the mixture in a bread loaf pan, and allow it to refrigerate uncovered for two hours. Serve whenever you like, and enjoy!

Rad Vegan Ricotta

Recipe Makes 2 cups.

Ingredients:

½ cup almonds
1 cup cashews
6 dates

1 cup water
1 tbsp. vanilla
1 ½ tbsp. lemon juice

Directions:

Begin by bringing the cashews, the dates, and the almonds together in a bowl. Pour in the wter, and allow the mixture to soak for thirty minutes.

Afterwards, bring the entire mixture along with the remaining ingredients into a blender, and blend the ingredients until the cheese is super creamy. Enjoy!

Eggplant-Based Vegan Queso

Recipe Makes 5 servings.

Ingredients:

8 1/3-inch thick eggplant rounds
salt and oil
3 tbsp. nutritional yeast
2 cups almond milk
1 tsp. cumin

½ tsp. minced garlic
2 tsp. cornstarch
1 tsp. chili powder
1/3 cup salsa

Directions:

Begin by slicing up the eggplant and salting it on both sides. Allow the eggplant rounds to sit in a colander in order to release moisture. Afterwards, pat them with towels.

Next, preheat your broiler to HIGH, and position your oven rack up top. Place the rounds on a baking sheet and pour a bit of olive oil overtop all of the rounds.

Broil the eggplant for five minutes. Flip the eggplants, and broil them once more for five minutes. Remove the eggplant from the oven.

After the eggplant has cooled, peel off the eggplant's skin. Pour the insides of the eggplant into a food processor with the rest of the ingredients—except for the salsa. Blend the ingredients until they're completely pureed.

Pour this mixture into a saucepan, and warm it up until it begins to bubble. Afterwards, remove the "cheese" and add the salsa. Position the cheese in a serving bowl, and enjoy with chips or crackers.

Vegan Blue Cheese Dressing

Recipe Makes 2 cups.

Ingredients:

1 cup vegan mayonnaise
1/3 block firm tofu
½ tsp. tahini

1 tsp. lemon juice
1 tsp. apple cider vinegar
½ tsp. garlic powder

Directions:

Begin by mixing together all the ingredients except for the tofu in a medium-sized bowl.

Next, crumble up the tofu into this bowl, and stir well. Serve this mixture with faux chicken nuggets or with crackers, and enjoy!

Vegan Mayonnaise

Recipe Makes 1 cup.

Ingredients:

½ cup soy milk
¾ cup canola oil
1 tsp. lemon juice

½ tsp. salt
½ tsp. mustard

Directions:

Begin by bringing the soy milk and the lemon juice together in a blender or a food processor.

As the milk and lemon juice blend together, add the oil. The mixture should thicken. Next, add the mustard and the salt.

Alter the seasoning if you so choose. Enjoy with various other recipes included in this book—including the vegan blue cheese dressing!

Flaxseed-Based Mayonnaise

Recipe Makes 1 cup.

Ingredients:

2 tbsp. flax seeds
½ cup almond milk
1 tsp. dry mustard
2 tsp. sugar
1 tbsp. white wine vinegar
½ tsp. salt
1 tbsp. lemon juice
1 cup grapeseed oil

1 tsp. onion powder

Directions:

Begin by mixing together the flax and the milk in a food processor or blender. The mixture should become frothy.

Afterwards, mix together the onion powder, the mustard, the sugar, the vinegar, the salt, and the lemon juice. Combine them into the food processor or blender, with the flax and milk.

Next, add the oil slowly. Blend for thirty seconds after you add just a little bit at a time. This gives your mayonnaise its desired consistency.

Enjoy!

Cashew-Based Vegan Sour Cream

Recipe Makes 1 ½ cups.

Ingredients:

1 cup cashews
2 tsp. lemon juice
3 tsp. apple cider vinegar

¼ tsp. salt
¼ cup water

Directions:

Begin by positioning the cashews in a small bowl and covering the cashews with boiling wate.r Allow the cashews to soak for forty-five minutes.

Afterwards, drain the cashews and pour them in a blender alongside the remaining ingredients. Puree the ingredients until you achieve your desired sour cream consistency. Enjoy!

Cashew-Based Vanilla Yogurt

Recipe Makes 1 ½ cups.

Ingredients:

1 cup cashews
¾ cup water

3 tsp. culture
1 tsp. vanilla

Directions:

Being by soaking the cashews in the water for two hours.

Next, drain he cashews and place the cashews in a food processor with about a tsp. of water until it's completely smooth. You can continue to add water to achieve your desired consistency.

Next, heat up this mixture in a saucepan over medium heat. Add the cultures and continue to stir. Afterwards, remove the mixture from the heat, and cover the mixture in a warm place for six hours.

After the mixture has curd, you can keep it in the refrigerator. Enjoy!

New Day Vegan Mozzarella Cheese

Recipe Makes 1 pound.

Ingredients:

1 cup nondairy yogurt (take out the vanilla of the recipe above)
1/3 cup canola oil
½ cup water
1 tbsp. carrageenan powder

2 tsp. salt
7 tbsp. starch
½ tsp. xanthan gum
9 cups chilled water

Directions:

Begin by bringing the yogurt, the oil, the water, and the salt together in a food processor. Process the ingredients until they're creamy. Next, pour the mixture into a glass bowl. Cover the bowl and allow the mixture to culture for twenty-four hours at room temperature.

Next, place the mixture in a saucepan and add the powder and the starch. Stir continuously for five minutes.

Next, pour very cold water and a bit of salt in a big mixing bowl. Stir the water. Next, formulate the cheese mixture into small balls. Drop the balls into the salted water, allowing them to harden nearly instantaneously.

Cover the water mixture and keep the cheese balls in the created water brine.

Vegan Swiss Cheese

Recipe Makes 2 ¼ cups.

Ingredients:

½ cup cashews
½ cup water
4 tbsp. lemon juice
1/3 cup nutritional yeast
2 tsp. Dijon mustard

2 tbsp. tahini
1 tbsp. dried onion flakes
1 tsp. garlic powder
1 tsp. ground dill
5 tbsp. agar flakes

Directions:

Begin by placing the cashews in water and allowing them to soak for two hours.

Next, place the cashews, the half cup of water, the nutritional yeast, the tahini, the lemon juice, the mustard, the garlic, the onion flakes, and the ground dill together in a food processor or blender. Puree the ingredients for about three minutes.

To the side, allow one cup of water to boil in a saucepan. Add the agar slowly, stirring continuously. After about one minute, place the heat on LOW, and allow the agar to simmer, stirring for about ten minutes.

Add the agar water to the blender or food processor a little bit at a time. Puree until the ingredients are completely smooth.

Next, pour this mixture into a container and set the container without a cover in the fridge.

After two hours, cover the cheese and allow it to chill for about eight hours. When it's done chilling, you can slice it and use it for things like the Vegan Reuben in a later chapter. Enjoy!

Vegan Thousand Island Dressing

Recipe Makes 1 ½ cups dressing.

Ingredients:

1 cup vegan mayonnaise
½ cup ketchup
½ tsp. onion powder

2 tbsp. sweet pickle relish
½ tsp. salt

Directions:

Bring all the ingredients together in a medium-sized bowl and serve with various dishes—like the Vegan Reuben! Enjoy.

Vegan Buttercream Frosting Recipe

Recipe Makes 3 cups.

Ingredients:

1 cup vegan butter
1 tbsp. soymilk
2 ½ cups confectioners' sugar
1 tsp. vanilla

1 tsp. apple cider vinegar
½ tsp. salt
1 tsp. vanilla
¼ tsp. almond extract

Directions:

Mix together the above ingredients, and spread the frosting over your favorite cakes and desserts. Enjoy.

Chapter 4:
Vegan for the Kids

Vegan Baby Cereal

Recipe Makes 1 serving.

ingredients

1/3 cup ground oats (ground in blender)
1 cup water

Directions:

Bring the water to a boil in a small saucepan. Add the ground-up oats to the water, and stir constantly.

Simmer the ingredients for a full twelve minutes, continuously stirring. Enjoy!

Vegan Baby Rice Cereal

Recipe Makes 1 serving.

Ingredients:

1/3 cup rice powder (brown rice in blender)
1 cup water

Directions:

Begin by boiling the water in a saucepan. When it begins to boil, stir the blended brown rice into the water, stirring all the time. Allow the ingredients to simmer for twelve full minutes as you continuously whisk.

Enjoy!

Baby's Barley Cereal

Recipe Makes 1 serving.

Ingredients:

1/3 cup barley ground in food processor
1 cup water

Directions:

Begin by boiling the water in a saucepan. Next, pour the grounded barley into the boiling water, and allow it to simmer for twelve minutes as you stir continuously.

Enjoy!

Too-Fun Tofu Fajitas

Recipe Makes 8 fajitas.

Ingredients:

8 flour tortillas
1 packaged baked tofu
1 cup vegan sour cream

1 cup salsa
1 ½ cups shredded lettuce
1 cup grated cheddar vegan cheese

Directions:

Begin by slicing the baked tofu into small strips. Microwave them for about three minutes on a microwave-safe plate. Position a bit of vegan sour cream and salsa in the center of the tortillas, and place tofu strips overtop of these ingredients. Add lettuce and cheese, and roll up the tortillas. Your kids will love them!

Enjoy.

McDonald's Enemy Tofu Chicken Nuggets

Recipe Makes 6 Servings.

Ingredients:

1 package extra-firm tofu
2 tbsp. corn meal

4 tbsp. wheat germ
1 tsp. salt

Directions:

Begin by preheating your oven to 400 degrees Fahrenheit.

Next, slice the tofu into ½-inch thick pieces. Blot at them with paper towel. Afterwards, make them into dice.

Mix together the cornmeal, the wheat germ, and the salt in a small bowl. Place the tofu dice in this bowl and completely coat them with the mixture.

Place the tofu on a baking sheet, and bake them for fifteen minutes. Make sure to stir them about three times during their baking in order to bake them completely. Serve the tofu with your kid's favorite sauce, and enjoy!

No-Cheese Mac-N-Cheese

Recipe Makes 8 Servings.

Ingredients:

10 ounces cavatappi pasta
1 package extra-firm tofu

2 cups non-dairy cheddar cheese
2 tbsp. vegan butter (from Earth Balance)

salt to taste

Directions:

Begin by cooking the noodles in boiling water until they're al dente. Immediately drain them and place them in a collinder.

Next, place the tofu in a food processor, and blend it until it's smooth. Place it in a saucepan along with the cheese and the butter, and allow the ingredients to simmer slowly. Stir continuously until the cheese is melted.

Next, mix together the macaroni and the created sauce, and season to taste. Enjoy!

Fruit and Faux Yogurt Morning Parfait

Recipe Makes 4 Servings.

Ingredients:

16 ounces non-dairy vanilla yogurt
2 cups sliced strawberries

sliced almonds
½ cup semi-sweet chocolate chips

Directions:

Begin by layering the yogurt followed by the fruit followed by the chocolate followed by the almonds. Repeat this layering until you've achieved your perfect parfait, and enjoy!

Children's Corn Chowder

Recipe Makes 8 Servings.

Ingredients:

1 diced onion
2 tbsp. olive oil
2 sliced carrots
1 diced celery stalk
2 cubes of vegetable bouillon
½ tsp. cumin

2 diced potatoes
3 cups frozen corn
1 package tofu
rice milk
salt and pepper to taste

Directions:

Begin by placing the olive oil in a large soup pot. Saute both the celery and the onions in the oil for five minutes.

Afterwards, add the potatoes, the carrots, the bouillon, and the cumin. Cover the ingredients with water, and allow the ingredients to simmer. After they begin to simmer, place the cover overtop, and allow the vegetables to simmer for an additional thirty minutes.

To the side, place the tofu in a food processor and completely blend it. Pour the pureed tofu into the vegetable mixture along with the frozen corn kernels. Next, pour rice milk into the chowder in order to give it a corn chowder-consistency.

Allow the mixture to simmer for fifteen more minutes. Salt and pepper the ingredients and enjoy!

Tempting Tofu Chocolate Pudding

Recipe Makes 4 Servings.

Ingredients:

1 package firm tofu
1 cup semi-sweet chocolate chips

1 tsp. vanilla
4 tbsp. agave nectar

Directions:

Blend the tofu in a blender of a food processor until it's creamy and smooth.

Next, place the tofu in a saucepan along with the chocolate chips. Cook this mixture over low heat, stirring continuously. The chocolate chips will melt.

Next, add the agave and the vanilla, and continue to stir. After two minutes, take the mixture off the stovetop and allow the mixture to cool completely. Chill prior to serving, and enjoy!

Winter Weather Tofu Scallops

Recipe Makes 6 Servings.

Ingredients:

8 red potatoes
1 sliced onion
3 tbsp. vegan butter

½ cup rice milk
1 package tofu
salt to taste

Directions:

Begin by baking the potatoes in a 400 degree oven for about twenty minutes. After the potatoes are cooled, skin them and slice them.

Next, position the oven to 375 degrees Fahrenheit.

Melt the vegan butter in a skillet, and sauté the onions in the butter.

To the side, pure the tofu in a blender or a food processor. Add the rice milk as the tofu purees.

Afterwards, bring the pureed tofu, the onions, and the sliced potatoes into a big mixing bowl. Toss the mixture together.

Next, position this mixture in a baking dish, and bake the mixture for forty-five minutes. Allow the mixture to cool for five minutes, and serve. Enjoy!

Sweet Carolina French Fries

Recipe Makes 4 Servings.

Ingredients:

6 Yukon gold potatoes
3 tbsp. olive oil
salt to taste

Directions:

Begin by preheating the oven to 425 degrees Fahrenheit.

Next, scrub the potatoes, and slice them into fries. Mix the fries with the olive oil, and position the fries onto a baking sheet. Allow them to bake for about thirty minutes, making sure to stir them around every few minutes. The potatoes should be crispy.

Enjoy!

Groovy Pizza Pie Potatoes

Recipe Makes 4 Servings.

Ingredients:

4 Yukon potatoes
1 ½ cups vegan mozzarella cheese

1 ½ cups marinara sauce
1 cup steamed broccoli

Directions:

Begin by completely baking the Yukon potatoes in the oven at 400 degrees Fahrenheit for about forty minutes.

After the potatoes have cooled, slice the potatoes in half. Go at the insides of the potatoes with a fork in order to fluff them up.

Next, spread marinara sauce over the potatoes and then add about 3 tbsp. of the vegan mozzarella cheese to each potato. Next, add broccoli. Bake the potatoes in the 400-degree oven for ten minutes. The cheese should be bubbling. Serve the potatoes instantly, and enjoy.

Macaroni Veggie-Loving Salad for Kids

Recipe Makes 6 Servings.

Ingredients:

10 ounces elbow macaroni
½ cup thawed green peas
½ diced red pepper
1 diced carrot
¼ cup thawed corn

½ cup vegan mayonnaise
2 tsp. pickle relish
1 tsp. mustard
salt to taste

Directions:

Begin by cooking the macaroni in boiling water until they're al dente. Afterwards, drain the macaroni and position the macaroni in a serving bowl.

Next, pour the vegetables into the macaroni, and stir well. Pour in the mustard and the mayonnaise, and stir well.

Salt the mixture, and serve either right now or later, after chilling. Enjoy!

Raising a Raisin Carrot Salad

Recipe Makes 6 Servings.

Ingredients:

8 peeled carrots
1 cup raisins
1 tbsp. agave nectar
1 tbsp. lemon juice
1/3 cup vegan mayonnaise
1 tsp. cinnamon

Directions:

Begin by grating up the carrots in a blender or a food processor. Next, position them in a glass bowl. Add the raisins, the nectar, the lemon juice, the vegan mayonnaise, and the cinnamon. Mix the ingredients well, and allow the mixture to stand for thirty minutes at room temperature. Afterward, serve and enjoy!

Picnic Ready Vegan Potato Salad

Recipe Makes 4 Servings.

Ingredients:

1 tsp. mustard

3 red skinned potatoes

½ cup vegan mayonnaise
½ diced red pepper
1 tbsp. apple cider vinegar

1/3 cup green olives
½ cup thawed green peas
salt and pepper to taste

Directions:

Begin by scrubbing the skins of the potatoes and baking the potatoes in the oven at 400 degrees Fahrenheit for about twenty-five minutes. Allow the potatoes to cool.

Next, dice up the potatoes into small chunks and position them in a serving dish. Place the rest of the ingredients into the serving dish, as well, and stir well. Serve either now or later, and enjoy!

Homemade Joyous Kid-Friendly Peanut Butter

Recipe Makes 1 ½ cups.

Ingredients:

1 cup peanuts
1 tbsp. agave nectar

1 tbsp. olive oil

Directions:

Position the peanuts in the food processor and allow them to completely puree. Next, add the agave and the oil and continue the process. You can make it smoother by adding more olive oil, if you like.

Position the peanut butter in a clean container, and store either in the refrigerator or in the cabinet. Enjoy!

Magic Morning Blueberry Muffins

Recipe Makes 12 muffins.

Ingredients:

2 tbsp. ground flaxseed
2 cups whole wheat flour
1 tsp. baking soda
2 tsp. baking powder
1 cup applesauce

½ cup sugar
1/3 cup vanilla soy milk
2 tbsp. safflower oil
1 tsp. cinnamon
1 cup blueberries

Directions:

Begin by preheating the oven to 350 degrees Fahrenheit.

Next, mix together the flour, the flaxseed, the powder, the soda, and the sugar together in a large bowl. Formulate a hole in the center, and add the wet ingredients. Stir well until you've created a dough.

Next, add the blueberries, and continue to stir for a thorough combination.

Pour the muffin batter into muffin tins, and bake the muffins for twenty-five minutes. The tops should be golden. Enjoy!

School Lunch Vegan Wrap

Recipe Makes 1 Serving.

Ingredients:

1 whole grain tortilla
½ sliced avocado

2 sliced sun-dried tomatoes
½ cup hummus

Directions:

Position the hummus in the center of the tortilla, and add the avocado and the sun-dried tomato overtop. Wrap up the tortilla, and then secure it with aluminum foil. Enjoy at school!

School Lunch Onion and Tempeh Wrap

Recipe Makes 1 wrap.

Ingredients:

1 tortilla
½ tsp. olive oil
½ diced onion

½ diced green pepper
3 ½-inch strips sautéed tempeh
dressing of choice

Directions:

Pour the olive oil into a skillet, and heat the onions in the oil for five minutes. Next, add the tempeh to the oil, and sauté the ingredients for about five more minutes.

Next, place the tortilla on a clean surface. Place the dressing of choice in the center followed by the sautéed tempeh, the onion, and the green pepper. Roll up the wrap, and secure the wrap with aluminum foil. Enjoy.

Vegan Groovy Elvis Sammie

Recipe Makes 1 Sandwich.

Ingredients:

3 sliced tempeh strips

½ tsp. olive oil

½ cup homemade peanut butter

½ sliced banana

2 pieces of whole wheat bread

Directions:

Begin by pour the olive oil in a skillet. Cook the tempeh in the skillet for about seven minutes, making sure to crisp it on both sides.

Next, spread out the peanut butter on both pieces of whole wheat bread. Place the banana slices on one piece and the tempeh on the other, and bring the bread pieces together.

Now, grill up the sandwich in the skillet to your desired golden-brown color. Enjoy!

No-Egg, Yes-Way Egg Salad

Recipe Makes 6 Servings.

Ingredients:

1 diced celery stalk

16 ounces firm tofu

1/3 cup vegan mayonnaise

1 diced scallion

1 tsp. curry powder

2 tsp. yellow mustard

3 tbsp. nutritional yeast

salt and pepper to taste

Directions:

Begin by slicing and dicing the tofu. Blot the tofu well on paper towels. Afterwards, place the tofu in a food processor, and puree the tofu well.

Next, place the tofu in a mixing bowl with the celery and the scallions.

To the side, mix together the mayonnaise, the curry powder, the nutritional yeast, and the mustard. Stir well. Pour this created mixture on top of the tofu, and mix well.

Season the mixture to taste, and enjoy between two pieces of bread or by its self.

Kiddie Quinoa Sloppy Joe

Recipe Makes 6 Servings.

Ingredients:

1 diced onion

1 tbsp. olive oil

½ cup quinoa

1 16-ounce can of red beans

½ diced green pepper

1 tbsp. low-sodium soy sauce

1 diced tomato

2 tsp. chili powder

1 tbsp. agave nectar

½ tsp. oregano

Directions:

Begin by bringing the quinoa together with a cup of water in a saucepan. Boil the ingredients together and then lower the heat to allow it to simmer for fifteen minutes.

Next, heat up the olive oil in a skillet. Saute the onions and the bell pepper.

Bring the rest of the ingredients into the skillet, and allow the mixture to simmer. Cook over medium, covered, for six minutes. Stir every minute or so.

Next, move the skillet from the heat, add the quinoa, stir, and allow the mixture to sit for five minutes.

Position the "sloppy joe" mix onto your favorite mini-pitas or vegan rolls, and enjoy.

Chapter 5:
Start Your Morning Right:
Very Vegan Breakfast Recipes

Super Vegan Pancakes with Pine Nut-Inspired Maple Syrup

Recipe Makes 3 Pancakes.

Ingredients:

1 cup whole wheat flour
1 cup cornmeal
1 ¾ cup water
1 tsp. salt
2 tsp. baking powder
1 ½ tbsp. olive oil

Syrup Ingredients:
1/3 cup agave syrup
1/3 cup maple syrup
2 tbsp. bourbon
1/3 cup pine nuts

Directions:

Begin by mixing together all of the pancake ingredients in a large bowl. Allow this mixture to sit together for fifteen minutes prior to cooking.

Next, oil a skillet and allow it to heat on medium heat. Next, portion about a fourth of the batter onto the skillet, and sauté both sides of the pancake, flipping carefully. Repeat this maneuver with all of the batter.

Next, mix together the syrup ingredients and pour this delicious mixture over the pancakes. Enjoy!

Morning Forest Maple Granola

Recipe Makes 4 ½ cups.

Ingredients:

2 cups oats
1/3 cup pumpkin seeds
1/3 cup sunflower seeds
1/3 cup walnuts
1/3 cup unsweetened coconut flakes

¼ cup wheat germ
1 ½ tsp. cinnamon
1 cup raisins
1/3 cup maple syrup

Directions:

Begin by preheating the oven to 325 degrees Fahrenheit.

Next, mix all of the above ingredients—except for the raisins and the maple syrup—together in a large bowl. After you've mixed the ingredients well, add the maple syrup, and completely coat the other ingredients.

Next, spread out this mixture on a baking sheet and bake the granola for twenty minutes, making sure to stir every four minutes or so. After twenty minutes, add the raisins and bake for an additional five minutes.

Remove the baking sheet and allow the granola to cool for forty-five minutes. Enjoy!

Vibrant Vegetable Tofu Scramble

Recipe Makes 3 Servings.

Ingredients:

1 diced onion
1 diced jalapeno pepper
1 chopped zucchini
1 chopped red pepper
1 diced tomato
1 tbsp. olive oil

1 tsp. turmeric
½ tsp. cumin
1 tbsp. nutritional yeast
1 package firm tofu
salt and pepper to taste

Directions:

Begin by pouring olive oil in a skillet and sautéing the jalapeno, the pepper, the zucchini, and the onion for about ten minutes.

Next, add the turmeric, the cumin, and the nutritional yeast, stirring well. Pour the diced tomatoes into the mix and continue to stir.

After you've completely removed the excess water from the tofu, crumble the tofu into the skillet with your fingers. Stir the scramble together, continuing to break up the mixture well. Salt and pepper the mixture, and enjoy.

Superfood Chia Seed Breakfast Bowl

Recipe Makes 2 Servings.

Ingredients:

1/3 cup chia seeds
2 tbsp. maple syrup
2 ¼ cups soymilk

1 tsp. vanilla extract
½ cup sliced bananas or fruit of your choice

Directions:

Begin by bringing together the chia seeds, the vanilla, and the soymilk in a serving bowl. Allow this mixture to sit together for thirty minutes. Afterwards, whisk the mixture and cover it, allowing it to chill overnight in the fridge.

In the morning, divide the mixture into appropriate serving sizes, and portion the banana overtop. Enjoy.

Arkansas Apple Oatmeal

Recipe Makes 1 Serving.

Ingredients:

½ cup rolled oats
1 tbsp. chia seeds
1 cored and peeled Gala apple
1/3 cup applesauce
1 tsp. cinnamon

1 cup almond milk
½ tsp. ginger
½ tsp. vanilla
1 tbsp. maple syrup

Directions:

Begin by mixing together the oats, the chia seeds, the apple, the almond milk, the cinnamon, the ginger, and the applesauce. Pour this mixture into a saucepan and allow it to heat over medium for ten minutes.

After the mixture begins to thicken, take the mixture off the heat and add the syrup and the vanilla. Pour this mixture into a bowl, and add any toppings you desire. Enjoy.

Silky Whole Wheat Strawberry Pancakes

Recipe Makes 24 pancakes.

Ingredients:

1 ¾ cup whole wheat flour
1/3 cup cornmeal
½ tsp. baking soda
1 tsp. baking powder
4 cups sliced strawberries

½ tsp. cinnamon
2 tbsp. maple syrup
2 cups vanilla soymilk

Directions:

Begin by combining all the dry ingredients together in a mixing bowl. Stir well, and create a hole in the center of the mixture in order to pour the syrup and soymilk into it. Continue to stir, making sure not to over-stir.

Next, add half of the strawberries into the mixture.

Heat the skillet or the griddle, and portion just a bit of Earth Balance butter overtop. Drop little pieces of the batter onto the skillet and cook both sides of the pancakes. Keep the pancakes warm as you cook the remainder of the batter, and top the pancakes with strawberries. Enjoy.

Grown-Up Vegan Chocolate Milk

Recipe Makes 3 cups.

Ingredients:

1/3 cup almonds
2 ½ cups water

1/3 cup maple syrup
1/3 cup cocoa powder

2 tsp. vanilla

Directions:

Begin by placing the water and the almonds together in a blender. Blend the mixture until the water is white and the almonds are meal-like.

Next, pour this mixture through a strainer, bringing the created water into a measuring cup. Toss out the almond meal.

Next, pour this almond milk back into the blender and add the remaining ingredients. Blend the mixture and continue to alter the ingredients to attain your desired sweetness. Enjoy!

Quinoa Sensation Early Morning Porridge

Recipe Makes 3 Servings.

Ingredients:

½ cup quinoa
3 tbsp. brown sugar
½ tsp. cinnamon

2 cups almond milk
½ cup water
dash of salt

Directions:

Begin by heating the quinoa in a saucepan over medium heat. Add the cinnamon, and cook the quinoa until it's sufficiently toasted. This should take about five minutes. Afterwards, add the remaining ingredients. Bring the mixture to a boil.

Next, place the stovetop to low heat, and allow the mixture to simmer for thirty minutes. If you need to, you can add more water if the porridge dries too quickly. Make sure to stir every few seconds.

Enjoy!

No-Egg Pop Eye's Spinach Quiche

Recipe Makes 6 Servings.

Ingredients:

1 container of tofu
2 minced garlic cloves
10 ounces spinach
1/3 cup soy milk
1/3 cup diced onion
1 cup shredded nondairy cheddar cheese
½ cup shredded nondairy Swiss cheese
½ tsp. salt

1 vegan pie crust

Directions:

Begin by preheating the oven to 350 degrees Fahrenheit.

Next, mix together the soymilk and the tofu in a blender until they're completely smooth. Add the salt and pepper.

To the side, mix together the garlic, the spinach, the onion, the "cheddar," the "Swiss," and the created tofu and milk mixture. Stir this mixture well, and pour the mixture into the vegan pie crust

Next, bake the quiche for thirty minutes in the preheated oven. Allow the quiche to set for five minutes after baking prior to serving. Enjoy!

Carrotastic Apple Muffins

Recipe Makes 12 Servings.

Ingredients:

2 ¾ cups all-purpose flour
4 tsp. baking soda
1 cup brown sugar
1/3 cup white sugar
4 tsp. cinnamon
2 tsp. salt
1 tsp. baking powder
2 ½ cups grated carrots
2 cored, peeled, and shredded apples
1 1/3 cups applesauce
1/3 cup vegetable oil
6 tsp. dry egg replacer

Directions:

Begin by preheating your oven to 375 degrees Fahrenheit.

Next, mix together the two sugars, the baking soda, the baking powder, the flour, the cinnamon, and the salt. Stir well.

To the side, mix together the applesauce, the egg substitute, and the oil. Stir well, and add the dry ingredients to the wet ingredients. Spoon this created mixture into muffin tins, and bake the muffins for twenty minutes. Allow them to cool prior to serving, and enjoy!

Vegan Variety Poppy Seed Scones

Recipe Makes 12 servings.

Ingredients:

1 cup white sugar
2 cups flour
juice from 1 lemon
zest from 1 lemon
4 tsp. baking powder

½ tsp. salt
1 cup Earth balance or vegan butter
2 tbsp. poppy seeds
½ cup soymilk
1/3 cup water

Directions:

Begin by preheating the oven to 400 degrees Fahrenheit.

Next, mix together the sugar, the flour, the powder, and the salt in a big mixing bowl. Add the vegan butter to the mixture and cut it up until you create a sand-like mixture. Next, add the lemon juice, the lemon zest, and the poppy seeds. Add the water and the soy milk, and stir the ingredients well.

Portion the batter out over a baking sheet in about ¼ cup portions. Allow the scones to bake for fifteen minutes, and let them cool before serving. Enjoy.

Vegan French Crepes

Recipe Makes 4 Servings.

Ingredients:

1/3 cup soymilk
2 tbsp. maple syrup
1/3 cup water
1 cup all-purpose flour

1/3 cup vegan butter or Earth balance
1 tbsp. sugar
½ tsp. salt

Directions:

Begin by mixing together all the above ingredients in a large mixing bowl and allowing it to chill for two hours.

Next, grease a skillet with vegan butter, and heat the skillet until it's very hot to the touch. Bring about 3 tbsp. of batter into the skillet and cook both sides, flipping carefully. Enjoy with your favorite fruity filling.

Homemade Raisin Rice Pudding

Recipe Makes 4 Servings.

Ingredients:

1 cup soymilk
1 cup water
½ cup diced and toasted almonds
3 ½ cups cooked brown rice

½ cup raisins
1 tsp. cinnamon
1/3 cup maple syrup
½ tsp. cardamom

Directions:

Begin by mixing together the cooked rice, the maple syrup, the raisins, the soymilk, the cinnamon, the almonds, and the cardamom in a saucepan. Allow the mixture to boil over high heat.

Next, place the heat on low and allow the mixture to simmer for nine minutes. Serve the pudding immediately, and enjoy!

Spiced Holiday Cranberry Oatmeal

Recipe Makes 1 serving.

Ingredients:

5/8 cup rolled oats
½ tsp. turmeric
½ tsp. ginger
1 tsp. cinnamon

1/3 cup dried cranberries
½ cup frozen blueberries
1/3 cup orange juice
1 cup water

Directions:

Begin by bringing all the ingredients—except for the orange juice—together in a saucepan and cooking the ingredients on high until the mixture begins to boil. Immediately place the heat on low and allow the mixture to simmer for about seven minutes. Afterwards, take the oatmeal off the heat and add the orange juice. Enjoy.

Spelt Flour Banana Muffins

Recipe Makes 12 muffins.

Ingredients:

1 ¾ cup spelt flour
2 mashed bananas
1 cup oats
½ cup olive oil

2 tsp. baking soda
½ cup white sugar
1 tsp. cinnamon

Directions:

Begin by preheating the oven to 350 degrees Fahrenheit.

Next, stir together the dry ingredients in a large mixing bowl. Add the mashed bananas, the sugar, and the oil one at a time. Stir until just moistened. Next, pour the batter into muffin tins, and bake the muffins for eighteen minutes. Allow the muffins to cool prior to serving, and enjoy.

Make-Your-Own vegan Muesli

Recipe Makes 8 cups.

Ingredients:

5 cups
1 cup raisins
½ cup toasted wheat germ
1/3 cup diced walnuts

½ cup wheat bran
1/3 cup oat bran
¼ cup brown sugar
1/3 cup sunflower seeds

Directions:

Mix together all of the above ingredients well in a large bowl. Store this created mixture in a sealable location in a cool, dry place, and enjoy when you wish with a bit of soymilk!

Morning Glory Vegan Pumpkin Muffins

Recipe Makes 12 muffins.

Ingredients:

1 ¾ cup whole wheat flour
½ cup brown sugar
1 tsp. cinnamon
1 tsp. baking soda
1 tbsp. baking powder

½ tsp. salt
½ tsp. nutmeg
15 ounce can of pumpkin
1/3 cup water
¾ cup chocolate chips

Directions:

Begin by preheating your oven to 375 degrees Fahrenheit.

Next, mix together all the dry ingredients in a large mixing bowl. Afterwards, add the wet ingredients and stir the mixture until it's just moistened. Pour the chocolate chips into the batter, and fold them to assimilate into the mixture.

Portion the batter into the muffin tins, and allow the muffins to cook for thirty minutes. Allow them to cool prior to serving, and enjoy!

Savory Breakfast Indian Flatbread

Recipe Makes 4 Servings.

Ingredients:

2 cups white rice flour
2 tsp. green chili peppers
½ cup green mung beans

1 cup water
½ tsp. asafetida powder
½ tsp. cumin seeds

1/3 cup shredded coconut
1/3 cup shredded carrot

3 tbsp. chopped cilantro
1/3 cup vegetable oil

Directions:

Begin by placing the mung beans in a bowl of water and allowing them to chill overnight. Remove the beans from the water on the next day and keep the leftover bean water.

Next, mix together the beans, the cumin seeds, the flour, the green chilies, the cilantro, the asafetida, the carrot, and the coconut. Stir the mixture well, and then add the water at a gradual rate. You can even mix with your hands to achieve a dough-like consisteny.

Next, make the dough into small balls and flatten them a bit at the top.

Heat up 2 tbsp. of the olive oil in a skillet over medium. Place the balls in the oil and fry them for about one minute on each side, flattening them out as you go. Continue to add oil to the skillet as you work through the dough balls, and serve the flat bread warm.

Enjoy!

Arabic Kidney Bean Breakfast

Recipe Makes 4 Servings.

Ingredients:

2 16-ounce cans of kidney beans
3 tbsp. olive oil
1 diced onion
2 tsp. cumin
1 diced jalapeno pepper

1 tsp. curry powder
1 diced tomato
3 tsp. tomato paste
salt and pepper to taste

Directions:

Begin by pour the olive oil in a skillet and heating it over medium. Add the onion, and cook the onion for five minutes. Next, add the jalapeno, and cook for an additional five minutes. Add the tomato paste and the tomato, and stir well in the skillet.

Afterwards, pour the kidney bean cans with their included liquid into the skillet. Add the curry powder and the cumin, and allow the mixture to boil, stirring continuously.

After it begins to boil, place the heat on low and allow the mixture to simmer for fifteen minutes. Enjoy.

Date and Walnut Muffins

Recipe Makes 12 muffins.

Ingredients:

1 cup cashew flour
2 tbsp. coconut flour
1 ½ cups diced dates
1/3 cup chia seeds
1 cup diced walnuts
1/3 cup ground flax seed
1 tsp. cinnamon

1 tsp. baking soda
1 ½ tbsp. tapioca starch
1/3 cup applesauce
1 ½ cups shredded zucchini
2 tbsp. melted coconut oil
1 tsp. sugar

Directions:

Begin by preheating the oven to 375 degrees Fahrenheit.

Next, place the chia seeds in a bowl of water and all the chia seeds to thicken for ten minutes.

Afterwards, stir together all the dry ingredients. Next, add the walnuts, the dates, the chia seeds, the applesauce, the zucchini, the coconut oil, and the sugar. Stir well, and spoon the batter into the muffin tins.

Bake the muffins for thirty-five minutes. Allow the muffins to cool prior to serving, and enjoy.

Blackberry Morning Smoothie

Recipe Makes 2 servings.

Ingredients:

1 cup almond milk
1 diced banana
½ cubed melon

4 tbsp. wheat germ
½ cup blackberries
5 ice cubes

Directions:

Bring all the above ingredients together in a blender, and blend the ingredients until you reach desired smoothie consistency. Enjoy!

Vegan Tropical Pina Colada Smoothie

Recipe Makes 1 smoothie.

ingredients

¾ cup soymilk
½ cup coconut milk
1 banana
1 ½ tbsp.. ground flax seed

1 tsp. vanilla
1 cup pineapple
1 tbsp. agave nectar
3 ice cubes

Directions:

Bring all the above ingredients together in a blender, and blend the ingredients to achieve your desired smoothie consistency. Enjoy!

Enriching Oatmeal Strawberry Smoothie

Recipe Makes 2 servings.

ingredients

14 strawberries
1 ½ cups soy milk
1 tsp. vanilla

1 banana
¼ cup oats
1 tsp. sugar

Directions:

Begin by bringing all the ingredients together in a blender and blending the ingredients to achieve desired consistency. Enjoy!

Mango Chia Smoothie

Recipe Makes 1 Smoothie.

Ingredients:

1 peeled and chopped mango
1 sliced banana
1 tsp. flax seeds
½ tbsp. chia seeds

1 cup water
½ cup romaine lettuce
3 ice cubes

Directions:

Begin by bringing all the above ingredients together in a blender and blending them until they've reached your desired smoothie consistency. Enjoy!

Chapter 6:
Lunch-Ready Vegan Wraps

Garbanzo Bean Naan Wrap

Recipe Makes 4 Servings.

Ingredients:

4 pieces naan bread
15 ounces chickpeas
½ diced onion
½ cup hummus
2 minced garlic cloves

1 sliced cucumber
1 cup spinach
5 slices of tomato
1 tsp. cumin

Directions:

Begin by mashing together the chickpeas, the hummus, and the other vegetable ingredients with a potato masher. Next, add the cumin, and continue to mash.

Bring the ingredients into a heated piece of naan, and roll the naan up into a wrap. Enjoy.

Mushroom Rice Noodle Wrap

Recipe Makes 4 Servings.

Ingredients:

½ pound shiitake mushrooms
2 minced garlic cloves
1 tsp. canola oil
2 tsp. soy sauce
4 ounces thin rice noodles

2 sliced avocadoes
1 sliced pepper
1 torn head of lettuce
2 peeled carrots
14 rice papers

Directions:

Begin by placing each of the rice papers out on a clean, dry surface.

To the side, place the canola oil, the garlic, the mushrooms, the peppers, the cooked noodles, and the soy sauce together in a skillet. Cook the ingredients for about ten minutes on medium-high, stirring constantly.

Layer this mixture into each of the rice papers, and top the ingredients with avocadoes, lettuce, and carrots. Roll the rice papers up into wraps, and enjoy!

Chinese-Inspired Vegan Wrap

Recipe Makes 4 Servings.

Ingredients:

1 package firm tofu

2 tbsp. soy sauce

2 cups cooked broccoli
3 cups sliced mushrooms
1 cup sliced onions
2 minced garlic cloves

1 tsp. olive oil
1 tsp. ginger
8 flour tortillas
½ tsp. crushed red pepper

Directions:

Completely remove the water from the firm tofu and allow it to dry out on paper towel.

Next, place the olive oil in a skillet, and cook the broccoli, the mushrooms, the onions, the soy sauce, and the garlic together for eight minutes, stirring all the time. Next, add the ginger and the tofu, and allow the tofu to become crispy. Administer the crushed red pepper, stir, and take the mixture off the heat.

Pour this mixture into the flour tortillas, and roll the tortillas tightly. Enjoy!

Foodie Lover's Lettuce Wrap

Recipe Makes 6 Servings.

Ingredients:

6 large lettuce leaves
2 diced tomatoes
3 tbsp. crushed pumpkin seeds
1 tbsp. raisins
3 tbsp. lemon juice

½ cup sprouts
1 sliced red pepper
3 minced garlic cloves
1 tbsp. apple cider vinegar
1 tbsp. water

Directions:

Bring the red pepper, the garlic, the pumpkin seeds, the lemon juice, and the sprouts together in a skillet along with the apple cider vinegar. Stir the ingredients and heat them on medium-high for about seven minutes. The sprouts should be wilted, and the garlic should be fragrant.

Next, spread out the lettuce leaves. Take the skillet off the heat and mix the remainder of the ingredients. Pour the ingredients into the lettuce wraps, and wrap up the lettuce. Enjoy.

Acing Avocado Rice Rolls

Recipe Makes 4 Servings.

Ingredients:

1/3 cup olive oil
1/3 cup oregano
1/3 cup parsley

2 minced garlic cloves
1/3 cup toasted and diced hazelnuts
1 cup cooked and cold brown rice

1 sliced avocado
1 package sliced tofu

8 rice paper wrappers

Directions:

Begin by combining the parsley, garlic, oregano, and olive oil together in a food processor. Pulse well, and place the sauce to the side.

Next, bring together the hazelnuts and the rice in a small bowl.

Boil some water, and place the boiling water directly next to you as you assemble your rice rolls. Dip the rice wrappers in the water for about four seconds, and then place the wrappers on a cutting board. Place rice at the bottom of the wrapper followed by the sauce; followed by a tofu strip; followed by avocado slices. Roll up the rice wrappers, and repeat the steps for the other rice wrappers and ingredients.

Enjoy!

Lentil Tahini Lettuce Wraps

Recipe Makes 6 Servings.

Ingredients:

9 whole-wheat tortillas
½ cup red lentils
2 tbsp. olive oil
2 cups water
1 cup bulgar

1 ½ tsp. red pepper flakes
1 diced scallion
1 cup red pepper paste
1 ½ cups shredded cabbage
1/3 cup tahini

Directions:

Begin by bringing the water and the lentils together in a saucepan. Cook the lentils over medium heat, and allow the mixture to boil for twenty minutes.

Next, remove the pan from the heat and add the bulgar. Allow the mixture to stand together for thirty minutes.

To the side, mix together the olive oil, the red pepper flakes, the red pepper paste, and the onions. Cook until they're soft, and add the cumin and the red pepper flakes. Cook for an additional minute.

Next, add the onion mixture, the scallions, and a bit of salt to the lentil mixture. Allow this mixture to cool, and then portion the mixture into the wheat tortillas. Add the shredded cabbage and the tahini, and roll the tortilla up into a wrap. Enjoy.

Black Bean and Sweet Potato Wrap

Recipe Makes 4 Servings.

Ingredients:

3 cups diced sweet potatoes
3 tsp. cumin
1 tbsp. olive oil
3 cups diced tomatoes

1 cup frozen corn
1 15-ounce can black beans
1 diced red pepper
4 whole-wheat tortillas

Directions:

Begin by preheating your oven to 400 degrees Fahrenheit.

To the side, bring the sweet potatoes together with the cumin and the oil, and toss them in a bowl. Place the potatoes on a baking sheet, and bake them for thirty minutes.

While this is happening, bring the black beans, the corn, the tomatoes, and the red pepper to a saucepan, and cook the mixture for twelve minutes on medium.

Next, place each tortilla on a plate and portion a bit of the potatoes and a bit of the bean mixture into the tortilla. Next, fold up the wrap, and enjoy.

California-Based Hummus Wrap

Recipe Makes 4 Servings.

Ingredients:

4 tortilla wraps
½ cup corn
4 tbsp. hummus
1 cup drained black beans

1 diced avocado
1 diced tomato
1 cup chopped lettuce

Directions:

Place the tortilla wraps out on plates, and place each of the ingredients together in the tortillas, evenly portioned. Roll the tortillas up into a wrap, and enjoy!

Winter Garlic Spring Rolls

Recipe Makes 4 Servings.

Ingredients:

12 rice papers
2 sliced onions
3 tbsp. ginger
5 tbsp. sunflower oil
1 package firm tofu
4 minced garlic cloves

8 ounces sliced mushrooms
1 cup chopped cilantro

Directions:

Begin by removing the tofu from the package and squeezing it to remove all the excess water. Next, slicing and dice the tofu, and place the tofu, the onions, the garlic, and the mushrooms together in a skillet on medium heat.

Stir and cook the mixture for about ten minutes. Afterwards, dd the ginger and the cilantro, and allow this mixture to cook for an additional three minutes.

Afterwards, administer the ingredients into the bottom of dampened rice papers, and roll the papers up into wraps. Enjoy.

Curried Potato Wrap

Recipe Makes 6 Servings.

Ingredients:

2 pounds cubed potatoes
2 cups garbanzo beans
1 ½ tbsp. olive oil
3 tsp. mustard seeds
1 diced onion
5 minced garlic cloves
½ tsp. cinnamon

1 tbsp. ginger
1 tsp. garam masala
½ tsp. coriander
1 ½ tsp. cumin
1 cup peas
1 cup vegetable stock
6 large whole-wheat tortillas

Directions:

Begin by slicing and dicing the potatoes. Heat the oil in a skillet, and place the mustard seeds in the oil until they begin to pop. Next, add the onions, the spices, and the potatoes to the skillet, and allow everything to cook nicely for about five minutes.

Next, add the vegetable stock and stir. Cover the skillet and allow it to simmer for twenty minutes.

Next, toss the peas into the mix, cover once more, and allow the mixture to cook for five minutes.

Allow the mixture to cool for twenty minutes before spreading it in whole-wheat tortillas, and wrapping the tortillas. Enjoy!

Tofu and Spiced Nut Wrap

Recipe Makes 12 rolls.

Ingredients:

1 package cubed Thai-flavored tofu
3 tbsp. olive oil
2 tsp. ginger

3 minced garlic cloves
1 chop sliced mushrooms
½ cup diced water chestnuts

1 diced carrot
2 tbsp. tamari sauce
1 cup toasted and chopped walnuts

2 minced onions
12 round rice paper wrappers

Directions:

Begin by heating the olive oil, the ginger, and the garlic together in a skillet over medium. Next, add the tofu and the mushrooms to the mix and allow them to cook for two minutes. Toss in the water chestnuts and the carrots, and cook for an additional minute.

Net, add the tamari sauce, and cook for three more minutes. Add the onions and the nuts, stir once or twice, and then remove the skillet from the heat.

Place warm water in a bowl, and wet all of the rice wrappers for about ten seconds each before aligning them on a flat surface.

Next, place the filling in the rice wrappers, and roll up the rice wrappers. Enjoy!

Soy Sauce and Mushroom Tofu Lettuce Wrap

Recipe Makes 4 Servings.

Ingredients:

2 packages firm tofu
4 tsp. soy sauce
1 tsp. rice vinegar
1 tbsp. sesame oil

4 diced onions
15 ounces chopped mushrooms
10 lettuce leaves

Directions:

Begin by stirring the tofu with the soy sauce and the rice vinegar.

Next, heat a large skillet to medium, and add the sesame oil and the tofu to the skillet. Allow the tofu to brown for about five minutes. Next, place the heat to high and add the mushrooms. Cook this mixture for five more minutes. Add the green onions, and continue to stir.

Bring the above mixture into each lettuce leaf, and roll the lettuce leaves to serve. Enjoy.

Kale Cravings Wrap

Recipe Makes 1 Serving.

Ingredients:

1 whole-grain tortilla
½ sliced avocado

2 tbsp. hummus
½ cup sliced kale

1/3 cup sliced cucumber
1 tsp. sunflower seeds

3 tsp. sliced onions

Directions:

Bring all the above ingredients into the tortilla, and roll the tortilla to serve. Enjoy!

Homemade Vegan Flour Tortillas

Recipe Makes 10 tortillas.

Directions:

4 ½ cups whole wheat flour
1 tbsp. baking powder
½ cup olive oil

1 tsp. salt
2 cups cold water

Directions:

Begin by bringing all the above ingredients together in a large mixing bowl and stirring well. Begin to knead the dough with your hands in order to form a sort of dough ball. Allow this dough to sit, undisturbed, for ten minutes.

Next, remove a small palm-sized ball of dough, and roll that dough into a ball. Roll the dough into a very thin "tortilla," and brown the tortilla in a skillet in order to brown it on both sides. Repeat this procedure until you finish with your dough!

Homemade Vegan Corn Tortillas

Recipe Makes 10 tortillas.

Ingredients:

2 ¼ cups Maseca
½ tsp. salt
1 ¾ cup water

Directions:

Begin by mixing the above ingredients together well in a bowl to create a dough. Divide the dough into small balls, and cover each of the balls with a towel.

Next, take balls out one at a time and roll over them with the rolling pin. Cook the tortillas one at a time in a heated, oiled skillet, browning them for just about one or two minutes on each side. Store the tortillas in a Ziploc bag, and enjoy whenever!

Chapter 7:
Vegan Soups, Chilis, and Stews

Burst Your Belly Vegan Tortilla Soup

Recipe Makes 6 Servings.

Ingredients:

3 minced garlic cloves
1 tbsp. olive oil
1 diced onion
¾ cup quinoa
1 diced green pepper
32 ounces vegetable broth

1 diced zucchini
6 corn tortillas
1 16 ounce can of diced tomatoes
1 tsp. cumin
½ tsp. oregano
salt and pepper to taste

Directions:

Begin by heating the oil in a soup pan, and adding the garlic and the onion to the oil. Cook these for five minutes. Afterwards, add the quinoa, the broth, and the bell pepper. Bring this mixture to a boil. Afterwards, lower the heat and allow it to simmer for fifteen minutes.

Next, slice up the tortillas into small strips and heat them in a skillet with a little olive oil in order to toast them.

Now, add the zucchini, the cumin, and the oregano to the soup. Stir, and allow it to simmer for fifteen more minutes. Add salt and pepper, and serve warm with tortilla strips overtop. Enjoy!

Mediterranean Pasta Soup

Recipe Makes 8 Servings.

Ingredients:

1 diced onion
1 tbsp. olive oil
4 minced garlic cloves
1 diced carrot
32 ounces cannellini beans
1 diced celery stalk
32 ounces vegetable broth

16 ounces tomatoes
1 ½ tsp. Italian herbs
2 bay leaves
1 ½ cup peas
2 cups elbow macaroni pasta
1/3 cup minced parsley
salt and pepper to taste

Directions:

Begin by heating the oil in a large soup pot and adding the vegetables to the oil. Stir the vegetables until the onions are golden. Next, add the beans, the tomatoes, the broth, the seasoning, and the bay leaves. Bring this mixture to a boil. Afterwards, lower the heat, and allow the mixture to simmer for ten minutes.

Remove the soup from the heat and allow it to stand for one hour.

Next, cook the pasta in a saucepan with boiling water. Before serving, add the pasta and the peas to the soup, and allow the soup to boil once more. Add parsley, remove the bay leaves, and serve.

Enjoy!

Protein-Revving Lentil Vegetable Soup

Recipe Makes 8 Servings.

Ingredients:

3 minced garlic cloves
1 diced onion
3 tbsp. olive oil
2 sliced carrots
2 diced celery stalks
5 cups water

2 diced potatoes
1 tbsp. Italian herbs
1 ½ cups green lentils
2 tsp. paprika
16 ounces diced tomatoes
1/3 cup chopped cilantro

Directions:

Begin by heating the oil and the vegetables together in the bottom of a soup pot. Saute the vegetables for about ten minutes. Afterwards, add the water, the lentils, the potatoes, the seasoning, and the paprika. Stir, and allow the mixture to simmer for thirty minutes with the cover on.

Next, place the cilantro in the soup and allow it to simmer for twenty more minutes. Serve with a bit of salt and pepper, and enjoy.

Quizzical Quinoa Soup

Recipe Makes 6 Servings.

Ingredients:

1 diced onion
1 tbsp. olive oil
6 diced carrots
3 minced garlic cloves
1 cup quinoa
16 ounces pink beans
32 ounces vegetable broth

2 tsp. curry powder
1 tsp. paprika
2 tsp. curry powder
1/3 cup chopped dill
5 ounces spinach leaves
salt and pepper to taste

Directions:

Begin by heating the oil and the vegetables together in the bottom of a soup pot for about seven minutes.

Next, add the vegetable broth, the quinoa, the beans, and all the spices. Simmer this mixture for twenty minutes with the cover on.

Next, add the tomatoes and a bit more water to administer the proper soup texture. Cook the mixture for ten more minutes.

Next, add the parsley, stir for a few minutes, and then serve the soup instantly. Enjoy!

Autumnal Apple and Squash Soup

Recipe Makes 6 Servings.

Ingredients:

2 pounds diced butternut squash
2 tbsp. olive oil
3 diced and peeled apples
32 ounces vegetable broth
3 tsp. ginger

1 diced onion
1 tsp. cumin
1 ½ tsp. curry powder
2 cups soymilk
salt and pepper to taste

Directions:

Begin by preheating your oven to 375 degrees Fahrenheit.

Next, wrap the butternut squash with aluminum foil, and bake the squash for forty-five minutes. Next, set them to the side to allow them to cool. Afterwards, remove the seeds, and peel the skin off. Slice and dice the squash.

Bring the squash and the soymilk together in a food processor, and pulse the ingredients.

Next, pour the oil into the bottom of the soup pot. Add the onion and sauté the onion for five minutes. Next, add the apple, the broth, and the spices. Bring this mixture to a boil and then allow it to simmer on low for twelve minutes.

Next, puree this soup pot mixture in the blender or food processor, and place this back in the soup pot. Add the squash and the soymilk to the mixture, and stir well. Now, allow this soup to simmer for ten more minutes, and salt and pepper before serving. Enjoy.

Barley Country Living Soup

Recipe Makes 8 Servings.

Ingredients:

2 tbsp. olive oil
32 ounces vegetable broth
1 diced onion
2 diced celery stalks
4 diced carrots

1 ¼ cup pearl barley
12 ounces sliced mushrooms
1 tbsp. basil
2 cups soymilk
1/3 cup minced parsley

salt and pepper to taste

Directions:

Bring by heating the oil and the vegetables together in a soup pot for eight minutes.

Next, add the broth, the barley, and the spices to the mixture. Allow the mixture to simmer for fifty minutes with a cover on top. Make sure to stir occasionally. Next, add the soymilk, and season the soup with salt and pepper.

Make sure to allow the soup to rest for thirty minutes prior to serving in order to allow it to thicken. Enjoy.

Spicy Vegetable Soup

Recipe Makes 6 Servings.

Ingredients:

1 cup soaked cashews
5 cups vegetable broth
3 diced garlic cloves
1 tbsp. olive oil
4 diced carrots
1 diced red pepper
2 chopped celery stalks

1 diced sweet potato
1 28-ounce can diced tomatoes
1 tsp. basil
1 tsp. paprika
1 tsp. cumin
2 cups spinach
15 ounce can of black beans

Directions:

Begin by soaking the cashews in a small bowl with water for two hours.

Next, bring the cashews and the vegetable broth together in a food processor. Puree the mixture until it's smooth.

Next, heat the oil and the vegetables together for five minutes in a soup pot. Add the spices, and stir, cooking for about seven minutes. Next, add the vegetable broth, and continue to stir. Allow the soup to simmer for twenty minutes.

Next, salt and pepper the mixture, and serve the soup warm. Enjoy!

"Cheese" Vegetable Soup

Recipe Makes 10 cups.

Ingredients:

1 tbsp. olive oil
4 minced garlic cloves
3 chopped onions
1 cup chopped carrots

1 cup chopped celery
6 cups chopped broccoli
2 cups chopped squash
2 ½ cups chopped sweet potatoes

5 tbsp. nutritional yeast
½ tsp. cinnamon

salt and pepper to taste

Directions:

Begin by bringing the oil, the garlic, and the onion into the bottom of a soup pot, and sautéing the ingredients over medium.

Next, add the rest of the vegetables, and sauté the vegetables for about seven minutes.

Next, cover the pot and allow the vegetables to cook for an additional six minutes.

Afterwards, pour in the vegetable broth. Allow the soup to simmer for twenty minutes. Remove the soup from the heat, and allow the soup to sit for twenty minutes. Afterwards, place the soup in a blender, and place the nutritional yeast in the mixture along with the spices. Blend the mixture, making sure to keep the blender lid a bit off due to the heat of the soup.

Pour this soup into the soup pot, and adjust the seasoning to taste. Serve warm, and enjoy!

Red Quinoa and Black Bean Soup

Recipe Makes 6 Servings.

Ingredients:

1 ¼ cup red quinoa
4 minced garlic cloves
½ tbsp.. coconut oil
1 diced jalapeno
3 cups diced onion
2 tsp. cumin
1 chopped sweet potato

1 tsp. coriander
1 tsp. chili powder
5 cups vegetable broth
15 ounces black beans
½ tsp. cayenne pepper
2 cups spinach

Directions:

Begin by bringing the quinoa into a saucepan to boil with two cups of water. Allow the quinoa to simmer for twenty minutes. Next, remove the quinoa from the heat.

To the side, heat the oil, the onion, and the garlic together in a large soup pot. Add the jalapeno and the sweet potato and sauté for an additional seven minutes.

Next, add all the spices and the broth and bring the soup to a simmer for twenty-five minutes. The potatoes should be soft.

Prior to serving, add the quinoa, the black beans, and the spinach to the mix. Season, and serve warm. Enjoy.

October Potato Soup

Recipe Makes 3 servings.

Ingredients:

4 minced garlic cloves
2 tsp. coconut oil
3 diced celery stalks
1 diced onion
2 tsp. yellow mustard seeds
5 diced Yukon potatoes

6 cups vegetable broth
1 tsp. oregano
1 tsp. paprika
½ tsp. cayenne pepper
1 tsp. chili powder
salt and pepper to taste

Directions:

Begin by sautéing the garlic and the mustard seeds together in the oil in a large soup pot.

Next, add the onion and sauté the mixture for another five minutes. Add the celery, the broth, the potatoes, and all the spices, and continue to stir. Allow the soup to simmer for thirty minutes without a cover.

Next, Position about three cups of the soup in a blender, and puree the soup until you've reached a smooth consistency. Pour this back into the big soup pot, stir, and serve warm. Enjoy.

Sunny Orange Carrot Soup

Recipe Makes 6 cups.

Ingredients:

2 tsp. coconut oil
2 cups diced onion
4 minced garlic cloves
1 cup orange juice
2 pounds chopped carrots

6 cups vegetable broth
3 tbsp. grated ginger
1 cup cashews
salt and pepper to taste

Directions:

Begin by bringing the cashews into a bowl of water and allowing them to soak for one hour.

To the side, heat the oil, the onion, and the garlic together in a large soup pot. Cook this mixture for three minutes. Afterwards, add the orange juice, the carrots, the vegetable broth, and the ginger. Stir well, and simmer to soup for twenty minutes. Next, all the soup to cool for fifteen minutes.

To the side, drain the cashews and blend the cashews with the rest of the soup in a blender.

Next, pour the soup back in the soup pot, and test the seasonings. Serve warm, and enjoy.

Lentil Luxury Soup

Recipe Makes 4 Servings.

Ingredients:

5 minced garlic cloves
1 tsp. olive oil
1 diced onion
½ tsp. coriander
1 cup diced celery
1 tsp. cumin

½ tsp. cayenne pepper
6 cups vegetable broth
¾ cup red lentils
¼ cup black lentils
1 ¼ cup green lentils
salt and pepper to taste

Directions:

Begin by heating the oil, the garlic, and the onion in the bottom of the soup pot for eight minutes.

Next, add the celery and the spices. Cook for three more minutes.

Add the cooked or canned lentils to the soup pot, next. Pour in the broth and stir well. Next, allow the soup to simmer for forty-five minutes. Stir often. Salt and pepper the soup as you please, and serve warm. Enjoy.

Broccoli Cheddar Vegan Soup

Recipe Makes 4 Servings.

Ingredients:

1 diced onion
1 tsp. olive oil
1 cup diced celery
3 minced garlic cloves
2 cups chopped potatoes
5 cups chopped broccoli

4 cups vegetable broth
½ tsp. cayenne pepper
2 tbsp. nutritional yeast
1 cup vegan cheese sauce
salt and pepper to taste

Directions:

Begin by heating the onion, the garlic, and the oil together in a soup pot for about seven minutes.

Next, add the celery, the potatoes, and the broccoli to the pot. Allow them to cook for six minutes. Next, add the nutritional yeast, the broth, and the cayenne, and allow the soup to simmer for twenty minutes.

Next, pour the soup into a blender and blend the soup until it's nearly smooth. Add the vegan cheese in between purees and mix well.

Next, pour the soup back in the soup pot and adjust salt and pepper seasoning. Enjoy!

Curried Lentil Squash Stew

Recipe Makes 4 Servings.

Ingredients:

1 diced onion
1 tsp. olive oil
4 minced garlic cloves
4 cups vegetable broth

1 tbsp. curry powder
1 cup red lentils
4 cups pre-baked butternut squash
1 cup broccoli

Directions:

Begin by bringing the oil, the onion, and the garlic together in the bottom of a soup pot for five minutes on medium. Next, add the curry powder, and stir the ingredients for a few minutes. Add the broth and the lentils to the pot, and allow the mixture to simmer for ten minutes.

Next, add the pre-baked butternut squash and the broccoli to the mixture. Allow the soup to cook for ten minutes, stirring occasionally. Add salt, pepper, and curry powder to the mixture to your desired taste, and enjoy.

Vitamin C-Stocked Barley Soup

Recipe Makes 10 cups.

Ingredients:

2 diced onions
1 tbsp. olive oil
4 minced garlic cloves
4 diced green onions
2 diced zucchinis
1 diced yellow pepper
3 diced carrots

5 cups vegetable broth
20 ounces diced tomatoes
½ cup buckwheat groats
1/3 cup pearled barley
2 tbsp. lemon juice
3 tbsp. parsley
salt and pepper to taste

Directions:

Begin by heating the onion, the garlic, and the olive oil in the bottom of a large soup pot. Heat them for eight minutes. Next, add the spices and cook for an additional two minutes. Add the rest of the vegetables, and cook them for five more minutes.

Next, add the broth, the diced tomatoes, the buckwheat, and the barley. Allow the soup to simmer for twenty minutes. Make sure to stir it every few moments.

Next, add the lemon juice and the rest of the spices you desire. Cook the mixture for a few more minutes, stirring occasionally. Then, serve warm, and enjoy!

Apple and Carrot Ginger Soup

Recipe Makes 5 cups.

Ingredients:

1 diced onion
2 tbsp. olive oil
2 tbsp. ginger
3 minced garlic cloves

1 diced and peeled apple
2 pounds diced carrots
5 cups vegetable broth
1 tsp. nutmeg

Directions:

Begin by bringing the olive oil, the onion, and the garlic together in a soup pot. Allow them to cook together for about five minutes. Next, add the ginger, the carrots, and the apples, and cook for an additional five minutes.

Next, add the vegetable broth. Allow the mixture to boil. Then, reduce the heat, and allow it to simmer for twenty minutes.

Next, blend the ingredients together in a blender along with the nutmeg. Bring the mixture back into the soup pot, season to taste, and enjoy!

Indian-Inspired Spiced Broccoli Soup

Recipe Makes 5 cups.

Ingredients:

1 cup uncooked red lentils
1 tsp. cumin
1 cup diced onion
3 tsp. mustard seeds
5 cups chopped broccoli
3 tbsp. olive oil

5 cups vegetable broth
3 cups almond milk
2 tbsp. lemon juice
2 tsp. red pepper flakes
1 tsp. garam masala
2 tsp. turmeric

Directions:

Begin by placing the oil, the lentils, the onion, the cumin, and the mustard seeds in a large soup pot. Cook this mixture for ten minutes on low.

To the side, process the broccoli in a food processor, and pour the broccoli in the soup pot. Add the vegetable broth, and allow the soup to simmer for twenty minutes with the cover on. Afterwards, add the almond milk, the turmeric, the garam masala, the lemon juice, and the red pepper flakes. Stir well, and adjust your seasonings however you see fit. Enjoy!

Christmastime Calm Soup

Recipe Makes 6 servings.

Ingredients:

1 cup chopped carrot
1 diced onion
1 tbsp. olive oil
½ cup quinoa
4 minced garlic cloves
½ diced zucchini
6 cups vegetable broth

15 ounces diced tomatoes
1 tsp. curry powder
15 ounces black beans
1 tsp. nutmeg
1 tsp. cinnamon
3 cups spinach
salt and pepper to taste

Directions:

Begin by heating the onion, the garlic, and the oil in the bottom of a soup pot for five minutes on medium. Next, add the rest of the vegetables except for the spinach and sauté them for seven additional minutes.

Next, pour the vegetable broth into the soup pot and add the quinoa, the black beans, and all the spices. Bring this mixture to a simmer, and allow it to cook like this, covered, for twenty minutes.

Next, add the spinach and stir. Simmer for an additional forty minutes. Adjust the seasoning, and enjoy!

Mushroom Quinoa Soup

Recipe Makes 5 cups.

Ingredients:

1 cup quinoa
3 diced onions
2 ½ pounds diced mushrooms
5 minced garlic cloves

8 cups vegetable broth
2 tbsp. vegan Worcester sauce
salt and pepper to taste

Directions:

Begin by preheating the oven to 350 degrees Fahrenheit.

Next, prepare the quinoa by boiling it in water for twenty minutes.

To the side, add oil, onion, and garlic to the bottom of a pot, and sauté them for five minutes. Add the mushrooms and cook for fifteen minutes to remove the mushroom water.

Next, add the vegetable broth and all the seasoning to the soup. Simmer the soup for ten minutes.

Next, blend half of the soup in a blender and add it back to the pot. Add the cooked quinoa and stir well. Serve the soup warm, and enjoy!

Roasted Tomato and Onion Soup

Recipe Makes 6 cups.

Ingredients:

5 ½ pounds sliced tomatoes
3 minced garlic bulbs
1 diced onion
1 tbsp. olive oil
1 can coconut milk

2 tbsp. tomato paste
4 cups vegetable broth
1 tsp. salt
2 tsp. garam masala
½ tsp. black pepper

Directions:

Begin by preheating your oven to 400 degrees Fahrenheit. Next, place the tomatoes, the garlic bulbs, and the onion along a baking sheet, and roast the vegetables for thirty minutes. Afterwards, remove the vegetables and set them aside.

Next, place these pre-roasted tomatoes, this garlic, and the onion in a soup pot. Add the tomato paste, the coconut milk, and the vegetable broth. Stir.

Add all the seasoning, and all the soup to simmer for fifteen minutes.

Next, place the soup in a food processor or blender. Pulse the ingredients well, and serve warm. Enjoy.

Groovy Gazpacho Soup

Recipe Makes 6 cups.

Ingredients:

1 diced red pepper
2 pounds diced tomatoes
1/3 cup diced onion
1 diced cucumber
1 tbsp. lime juice
1 diced garlic cloves

1 tsp. salt
2 cups tomato juice
2 tbsp. chopped Parsley
1 tsp. olive oil
4 tbsp. red wine vinegar

Directions:

Begin by placing the pepper, tomatoes, cucumber, garlic, onion, lime juice, tomato juice, herbs, and olive oil together in a blender. Blend the ingredients until they're smooth.

Next, adjust the seasoning to your taste. Chill the soup for four hours in the fridge prior to serving. Enjoy!

Sweet Pie Strawberry Almond Soup

Recipe Makes 3 cups.

Ingredients:

2 pounds sliced strawberries
1/3 cup almond milk
3 tbsp. almond butter

1 tsp. almond extract
3 tbsp. agave

Directions:

Bring all the above ingredients together in a blender. Blend the ingredients until you reach your desired consistency, adding almond milk as needed.

Next, taste test the soup and add agave as needed.

Chill the soup in the refrigerator overnight, and serve cold. Enjoy!

Super Vegetable Vegan Chili

Recipe Makes 8 Servings.

Ingredients:

1 diced onion
1 tbsp. olive oil
1 ½ cups diced carrots
2 diced jalapeno peppers
½ cup bulgur
2 tbsp. chili powder
4 minced garlic cloves

2 cups diced tomatoes
1 tbsp. cumin
15 ounce can of kidney beans
15 ounce can of black beans
2 cups tomato paste
salt and pepper to taste

Directions:

Begin by heating the vegetables and the oil at the bottom of a soup pot. Saute this mixture for ten minutes. Next, add the chili powder, the bulgur, and the cumin. Stir well.

Next, add the tomato sauce, the diced tomatoes, and both beans. Allow the mixture to boil. Afterwards, reduce the heat of the mixture, cover the mixture, and allow the mixture to simmer for one hours. Season the chili to suit your tastes, and enjoy!

Vegan Mexicano Chili

Recipe Makes 8 Servings.

Ingredients:

1 diced carrot

1 diced celery stalk

1 tbsp. olive oil
1 diced onion
2 minced garlic cloves
1 tsp. cumin
1 tbsp. tomato paste
1 tsp. coriander
1 tsp. cumin

1 tsp. paprika
1 tsp. soy sauce
400 grams diced tomatoes
400 grams black beans
400 grams aduki beans
400 grams kidney beans

Directions:

Begin by placing the celery, onion, carrot, garlic, and oil in a large soup pot and cooking the vegetables for ten minutes, stirring occasionally.

Add the tomato paste, the cumin, the cumin, and the paprika. Stir well, and then add the diced tomatoes, the pepper, and the soy sauce.

Next, pour in all the canned beans, and allow the chili to simmer for twenty minutes. Enjoy!

Beer Rejoice Vegan Chili

Recipe Makes 8 Servings.

Ingredients:

1 diced onion
1 tbsp. olive oil
5 minced garlic cloves
½ diced green pepper

1 tbsp. chili powder
12 ounces Mexican beer like Negra Modelo
15 ounces kidney beans
15 ounces black beans

Directions:

Begin by pouring the oil in a soup pot and adding the garlic, the pepper, the onion, and the salt and pepper to the mixture. Stir and cook for eight minutes.

Next, add the chili powder and the beer. Cook well, and allow the mixture to reduce for ten minutes.

Next, add the beans, the tomatoes, and a bit of salt and pepper. Allow the chili to simmer for thirty-five minutes. Serve warm, and enjoy!

Vegan Sunny Potato Stew

Recipe Makes 4 Servings.

Ingredients:

1/3 cup white rice
1 diced onion

4 diced carrots
3 diced potatoes

1 diced turnip
1 diced parsnip
1 tsp. cumin

3 cups water
salt and pepper to taste

Directions:

Begin by combining together all of the above ingredients in a big soup pot over medium heat. Stir well, and boil for thirty minutes. Allow the soup to simmer for five additional minutes, stirring all the time. Salt and pepper the stew to taste, and enjoy.

Vegan Faux Chicken Noodle Soup

Recipe Makes 4 Servings.

Ingredients:

4 cups vegetable broth
1 diced celery stalk
1 cup sliced baby carrots
3 ounces broken pieces of fettuccine

1 diced onion
2 tbsp. textured vegetable protein (found at your local health food store)
1 tbsp. minced parsley

Directions:

Begin by bringing the vegetable broth, the celery, the carrots, and the onion together in a large soup pot. Bring it to a simmer over medium. Next, add the fettuccine, and cover the soup, allowing it to simmer for fifteen minutes.

At this point, add the vegetable protein and cook the soup for an additional five minutes. The vegetables and the noddles should be tender. Add the parsley before servings, and enjoy.

Vegan Faux Beef Stew

Recipe Makes 8 Servings.

Ingredients:

1 pound cubed and cooked seitan
4 tbsp. olive oil
1 minced garlic cloves
1 diced onion
14 ounces tomatoes

5 cups vegetable broth
7 diced carrots
3 chopped potatoes
10 ounces frozen green beans
3 tbsp. cornstarch

Directions:

Begin by sautéing the seitan in olive oil over medium heat.

Afterwards, add the listed olive oil, the garlic, and the onion to a soup pot. After five minutes of stirring and cooking on medium, add the tomatoes, the vegetable broth, the seitan, the salt, and the pepper. Allow the stew to simmer for one hour.

Afterwards, add the potatoes, the carrots, and the green beans. Allow the stew to simmer for thirty minutes more, and then thicken it up with the cornstarch. Allow the stew to simmer for ten more minutes before serving. Enjoy.

Sweet Potato Slow Cooker Chili

Recipe Makes 4 Servings.

Ingredients:

1 diced onion
5 minced garlic cloves
1 chopped green pepper
1 tbsp. cumin
1 tbsp. chili powder
½ tsp. cinnamon

3 tsp. cocoa powder
28 ounces diced tomatoes
1 can kidney beans
1 can black beans
1 peeled and diced sweet potato
1 cup water

Directions:

Begin by bringing together the pepper, the onion, the garlic, the cuin, the chili powder, the cocoa, and the cinnamon together in a slow cooker. Next, add the beans, the tomatoes, the sweet potato, and a cup of water.

Cover the slow cooker and cook for eight hours on LOW. Serve warm, and enjoy.

Extraordinary Slow Cooker Lentil Chili

Recipe Makes 8 Servings.

Ingredients:

1 diced onion
1 diced jalapeno
4 minced garlic cloves
1 chopped yellow pepper
1 diced carrot
2 15-ounce cans of tomatoes

2 15-ounce cans of tomato sauce
2 15-ounce cans red beans
16 ounces lentils
3 tbsp. chili powder
1 tbsp. cumin

Directions:

Begin by placing all the ingredients together in the slow cooker. Stir well, and cook the ingredients on LOW for seven hours. Serve the chili warm, and enjoy!

Chapter 8:
Tempting Tempeh
Recipes Galore

Make-Your-Own Tempeh

Recipe Makes 2 pounds tempeh.

Ingredients:

1 ½ pounds dry soy beans
5 tbsp. vinegar
1 ½ tsp. tempeh starter culture (found at Whole Foods, natural grocer, or Amazon)

Directions:

Begin by soaking the soybeans in 2 liters of water for twenty hours.

Next, place the beans in a large pot and cover the beans with water. Pour in the vinegar, and cook the beans for thirty minutes. Next, drain the water and dry off the beans by heating them in the large pot on medium. Allow the beans to completely cool.

Next, add the tempeh starter culture over the soybeans, and stir well.

Prepare two big, clean plastic bags by stabbing them with tiny holes with a needle. Position the soybeans in these two bags and seal the bags. Place the beans in a warm area of your home for two days. This allows the tempeh to ferment.

Afterwards, the bags should be filled with white mycelium, allowing you to lift the contents of the bag out all at once.

This is tempeh. From here, you should store it in a clean, sealable container in either your freezer or your refrigerator. Enjoy!

Ultimate Seeded Tempeh Cutlets

Recipe Makes 4 Servings.

Ingredients:

16 ounces tempeh
2 minced garlic cloves
2 tbsp. soy sauce
2 tbsp.. nutritional yeast flakes
1 tbsp. agave nectar

2 tbsp. Dijon mustard
1 ½ tbsp. sesame oil
4 tbsp. hempseeds
6 tbsp. sesame seeds
3 tbsp. chia seeds

Directions:

Begin by slicing the tempeh into ½-inch slices. Place these slices in a baking sheet.

To the side, mix together the nutritional yeast flakes, the vinegar, the garlic, the agave, the sesame oil, and the mustard. Stir well, and pour this mixture over the tempeh. Flip the tempeh in order to coat each side evenly. Place the tempeh baking pan in the refrigerator for four hours.

Next, preheat your oven to 425 degrees Fahrenheit. Place the seeds out on a plate, and then stir them together. Coat each piece of tempeh with the seeds, pressing the pieces down firmly in the seeds. Position the tempeh bake in the baking pan, and bake the prepared, seeded tempeh in the oven for twenty minutes.

Afterwards, flip the tempeh, and bake the tempeh for an additional twenty minutes. Enjoy immediately.

Asian-Inspired Tempeh Satay

Recipe Makes 3 Servings.

Ingredients:

1 diced onion
3 minced garlic cloves
1 sliced zucchini
3 cups broccoli
1/3 cup peanut butter

1/3 cup soymilk
3 diced tomatoes
8 ounces of sliced tempeh
3 cups chopped bok choy

Directions:

Begin by sautéing both the onion and the garlic together in a bit of olive oil for about seven minutes. Next, add the broccoli and the zucchini and sauté for an additional five minutes.

To the side, mix together the peanut butter and the soymilk. Pour this mixture into the large pan. Next, add the tempeh slices, the tomatoes, and the bok choy. Continue to stir fry until you've reached your desired taste and texture. Enjoy!

Warm Winter Night Tempeh Stew

Recipe Makes 6 Servings.

Ingredients:

16 ounces cubed tempeh
2 tbsp. olive oil
¾ cup white wine
3 cups water
8 sliced mushrooms
2 ½ tbsp. mustard
2 cups chopped sweet potatoes

2 cups halved Brussels sprouts
2 cups chopped carrots
1 ½ tbsp. miso
2 tsp. sage
2 tsp. thyme
1 tsp. rosemary

Directions:

Begin by heating the olive oil in a large soup bot over medium. Next, add the tempeh to the oil and cook the tempeh until it's golden brown.

Pour in the wine, the water, and the mustard, and stir well. Add the mushrooms. Next, administer the sweet potatoes, the Brussels sprouts, the carrots, the onions, and the sprouts. Allow the mixture to boil. Afterwards, reduce the mixture to medium-low, and allow the mixture to simmer for twenty-five minutes.

Next, add the miso to the pot with the spices. Simmer for about five more minutes, stirring occasionally. Enjoy!

Smoked Tempeh

Recipe Makes 4 Servings.

Ingredients:

8 ounces sliced tempeh
2 tbsp. agave nectar
2 tbsp. soy sauce

3 tbsp. ketchup
1 ½ tbsp. olive oil
1 tsp. smoked paprika

Directions:

Begin by slicing the tempeh.

Next, combine the nectar, the soy sauce, the ketchup, the olive oil, and the smoked paprika together in a medium-sized bowl. Pour this mixture into a saucepan or skillet, and allow the mixture to heat over medium.

Next, place the tempeh strips in the sauce and cook the sauce and the tempeh for about ten minutes, flipping the tempeh after five minutes. Serve warm—either between pieces of bread or by themselves. Enjoy!

Tempeh Mexican Tamale Pie

Recipe Makes 4 Servings.

Ingredients:

16 ounces sliced tempeh
½ cup tamari
1/3 cup vegetable broth
1/3 cup rice vinegar
2 cups water
½ tsp. thyme

1/3 cup cornmeal
16 ounces salsa
14-ounces creamed corn (which is vegan, always)
½ sliced olives
1 sliced tomato

Directions:

Begin by placing the slices of tempeh in a baking dish. To the side, mix together the tamari, the vinegar, the broth, and the thyme. Pour this mixture over the tempeh, and allow the tempeh to marinate for two hours.

Next, preheat the oven to 400 degrees Fahrenheit.

Afterwards, place two tbsp. of the created marinade in a skillet along with the marinated tempeh. Cook the tempeh for about seven or eight minutes, flipping all the time to cook both sides.

To the side in a small saucepan, bring the two cups of water to a boil. Add the cornmeal. Next, place the heat to low, and cook for an additional three minutes, stirring continuously. Next, add the creamed corn and continue to stir. Cook for an additional ten minutes.

To the side, in a baking dish, bring together the tempeh, the olives, and the salsa. Add the cornmeal mixture to the baking dish, as well, and then top the mixture with the olives and the tomatoes.

Bake the mixture for twenty-five minutes to create a bubbly, delicious masterpiece. Serve warm, and enjoy!

Tropical Pineapple Tempeh with Green Beans

Recipe Makes 8 Servings.

Ingredients:

20 ounces sliced and diced tempeh
½ cup hoisin sauce
2 tbsp. olive oil
1/3 cup orange juice
2 tbsp. soy sauce

3 tbsp. lemon juice
½ diced grilled pineapple
12 ounces green beans
2 sliced red peppers

Directions:

Begin by bringing together the sauce, the olive oil, the orange juice, the soy sauce, and the lemon juice in a small bowl. Stir well, and set the ingredients to the side.

Next, grill up the pineapple on the grill or in a skillet. Afterwards, set the pineapple in the serving dish.

Slice the tempeh and bring the tempeh into the bowl with the marinade. Place the coated tempeh on the grill or in the skillet over medium-high heat, and all the tempeh to become charred on both sides.

Position the tempeh alongside the grilled pineapple.

To the side, mix together the green beans and the bell peppers with a bit of the marinade. Toss the vegetables together, and place a layer of this vegetable goodness on the grill. Grill these vegetables for ten minutes. Place these ingredients alongside the tempeh and the pineapple, and serve warm. Enjoy!

Rambling Tempeh Reuben

Recipe Makes 1 Sandwich.

Ingredients:

1 slice of tempeh
1 tbsp. vegan thousand island dressing
1/3 cup sauerkraut

1 slice vegan Swiss cheese
½ tbsp. Earth Balance butter
2 sliced rye bread

Directions:

Begin by spreading Earth balance over one side of each piece of rye bread and heating a skillet over medium heat. Place the bread down on the skillet, and top the bread with the tempeh, the vegan cheese, the vegan thousand island, and the sauerkraut. Top the other piece of bread over the sandwich, and flip the sandwich until the bread is appropriately toasted and the cheese is melt-y. Enjoy!

Tempeh "Tuna" Salad

Recipe Makes 4 cups.

Ingredients:

1 tbsp. seaweed flakes
2 ½ cups vegetable broth
8 ounces tempeh
2 tbsp. lemon juice
1 ½ tbsp.. soy sauce

2 minced garlic cloves
1 cup diced celery
1 diced onion
1 cup diced dill pickles
1/3 cup vegan mayonnaise

Directions:

Begin by pouring the vegetable broth into a large saucepan and heating it on medium heat. Next, place the tempeh in the broth and allow the tempeh to simmer for twenty minutes. Drain the mixture and allow the tempeh to cool. Next, grate it up into smaller pieces in a big serving bowl.

Next, to the side, stir together the lemon juice, the soy sauce, the seaweed flakes, and the garlic. Add this mixture to the tempeh and stir well. Add the onion, the dill, and the celery, and toss the mixture with the mayonnaise. Chill the salad well prior to serving, and enjoy.

French Tempeh Ratatouille

Recipe Makes 4 Servings.

Ingredients:

8 ounces tempeh

2 chopped potatoes

14 ounce can of tomatoes
1 diced carrot
1 diced onion
8 ounce can of chickpeas
1 peeled and diced eggplant
2 diced garlic cloves

1 cup chopped broccoli
1/3 cup vegetable broth
½ cup chopped green beans
1 chopped zucchini
½ tsp. dried rosemary

Directions:

Begin by bringing the carrots, the potatoes, and the onion together in a big saucepan. Fill the pan with water to cover the vegetables, and allow the mixture to boil. Cover the mixture and place the heat on low. Simmer the mixture for five minutes.

Then, add the broccoli, the eggplant, the zucchini, and the green beans. Continue to simmer the mixture for two minutes, and then add the vegetable broth, the tempeh, the tomatoes, and the chickpeas. Cook the mixture for an additional ten minutes, and enjoy warm.

Good Morning Tempeh Bacon

Recipe Makes 4 Servings.

Ingredients:

1 tbsp. olive oil
2 tsp. tamari
8 ounces sliced tempeh

Directions:

Begin by placing the olive oil in a skillet, and placing the sliced tempeh in the oil until it's browned on both side. Add the tamari over the tempeh, and serve warm and slightly crispy for an awesome morning treat—or for Elvis Peanut Butter and Banana Sandwiches.

Fried Glory Garlic Tempeh

Recipe Makes 4 Servings.

Ingredients:

8 ounces tempeh
3 minced garlic cloves
2 cups olive oil

1 cup water
salt

Directions:

Begin by placing the water, the salt, and the garlic in a mixing bowl and stirring well.

To the side, slice the tempeh into 1-inch thick strips. Marinate the tempeh in the created marinade for about twenty-five minutes.

Afterwards, fry the tempeh in the olive oil, making sure to brown the tempeh on both sides. Enjoy.

Marinated Snow Pea Tempeh

Recipe Makes 4 Servings.

Ingredients:

2 tbsp. soy sauce
3 tbsp. apple cider
1 tsp. grated ginger
8 ounces sliced tempeh
3 tsp. coconut oil
8 ounce snow peas
1 shredded carrot
3 shredded cups cabbage

1/3 cup diced cilantro
1 diced onion
3 tbsp. white miso
4 tbsp. lemon juice
1/3 cup olive oil
1 tbsp. maple syrup
2 minced garlic cloves

Directions:

Begin by mixing together the soy sauce, the apple cider, the ginger, and the coconut oil in a bowl. Place the tempeh in the bowl, and allow it to marinate for three hours.

Next, bake the tempeh in the oven at 375 degrees Fahrenheit for twenty-five minutes.

Next, heat the snow peas in boiling water for thirty seconds before removing them and allowing them to cool in water.

Next, mix all the above ingredients together in a big salad serving bowl, toss to coat in the various juices, and enjoy.

Make Your Own Chimichurri with Tempeh

Recipe Makes 2 Servings.

Ingredients:

10 ounces sliced tempeh
4 minced garlic cloves
1 cup parsley
1 cup chopped cilantro
1/3 cup red wine vinegar
1 tsp. oregano
½ tsp. salt
½ tsp. red pepper flakes
3 tbsp. olive oil

1 cup vegetable broth
1 tbsp. soy sauce

Directions:

Begin by steaming the tempeh for eight minutes.

Afterwards, bring every other ingredient except for the soy sauce into a food processor and blend them until smooth.

Pour half of this created mixture into a separate cup, and add the tamari to this, stirring well.

Pour about 3 tbsp. of this mixture onto a plate, and place the tempeh on the plate. Pour the other half of the marinade over it, and rub the tempeh well. Allow the tempeh to rest for one hour. Afterwards, flip the tempeh and allow it to sit for twenty minutes.

Next, pour olive oil into the bottom of a skillet and cook the tempeh in the oil until you've achieved a golden brown color. Enjoy.

Comfort Food Grilled Cheese with Tempeh

Recipe Makes 2 sandwiches.

Ingredients:

4 ounces sliced tempeh
2 tbsp. water
½ tsp. olive oil
½ tsp. curry powder
4 slices sourdough bread

1 tsp. vegan butter
4 slices vegan cheese of your choice
1 cup spinach
2 tbsp. apricot preserves

Directions:

Begin by slicing the tempeh and marinating it with the soy sauce, the water, and the curry powder. Make sure to coat the tempeh.

Cover the tempeh and allow it to marinate for one hour.

Next, heat oil in a skillet and fry the tempeh. Flip and brown the tempeh.

Make the grilled cheese by grilling the vegan buttered bottom of both pieces of bread with the tempeh and the cheese positioned on one half. Add the vegan cheese and the spinach, and then place the non-ingredient-laden piece of bread on the sandwich. Flip the sandwich and make sure the vegan cheese melts. Enjoy immediately.

Tropical Coconut Tempeh with Kale

Recipe Makes 6 Servings.

Ingredients:

2 cups torn kale

2 diced onions

2 limes
1 tbsp. olive oil
2 cups cilantro
1 bulb of lemongrass
1 diced green chili

2-inch diced piece of ginger
½ cup coconut milk
1 tsp. soy sauce
2 tbsp. coconut oil
8 ounces diced tempeh

Directions:

Begin by bringing together the greens, the cilantro leaves, the lime, a bit of olive oil, and salt and pepper in a large boil. Toss these ingredients well.

Next, slice zest from one of the limes and slice it up. Grind tem in a mortar and pestle with some onion.

Next, slice up the lemongrass bulb, the ginger, and the chili, and grid these, as well. Lastly, create a paste of these ingredients by adding droplets of lime juice. After the paste has been achieved, pour the mixture into a small bowl. Add the coconut milk and the soy sauce. Add the remaining cilantro and stir well.

To the side, heat the coconut oil and add the rest of the onions. Next, add the tempeh and stir well for about eight minutes.

Next, bring all the ingredients together in a serving bowl, and enjoy!

Cucumber with Tempeh Skewers

Recipe Makes 1 Serving.

Ingredients:

½ cup diced tempeh
¾ cup diced cucumber

Directions:

Begin by sautéing the tempeh in a bit of olive oil in a skillet. Next, add a bit of salt and pepper. Skewer the tempeh and the cucumber with a toothpick or a large skewer, and enjoy!

Hummus and Tempeh Sandwich

Recipe Makes 4 Servings.

Ingredients:

10 ounces tempeh
3 tbsp. soy sauce
1 tbsp. agave
2 tbsp. apple cider vinegar
2 tsp. olive oil

2 tsp. paprika
8 slices whole grain bread
1/3 cup hummus

Directions:

Begin by stirring together the soy sauce, the agave, the vinegar, the paprika, and the olive oil. Marinate the tempeh in the marinade, and allow it to sit for three hours.

Next, preheat the oven to 350 degrees Fahrenheit, and bake the tempeh for thirty minutes.

Next, prepare the sandwich by placing a layer of hummus over one piece of bread, placing the tempeh overtop, and topping the tempeh with whatever ingredients you like on your sandwiches. Enjoy!

Chermoula Chipper Tempeh Munchers

Recipe Makes 12 Servings.

Ingredients:

7 tbsp. olive oil
3 cups vegetable broth
1 ¼ pound cubed tempeh

2 cups chermoula
½ tsp. salt

Directions:

Begin by preheating the oven to 350 degrees Fahrenheit.

Next, heat the olive oil in a skillet and cook the tempeh in the skillet for five minutes. Cook the tempeh for five minutes on the opposite side. Do this for all six pieces of tempeh.

Next, bring the chermoula, the broth, and the salt together in a saucepan. Allow the mixture to boil. Next, pour the mixture over the tempeh, and position the tempeh in a baking dish. Cover the tempeh with aluminum foil and allow it to marinate for two hours.

Next, remove the foil and bake the tempeh for fifteen minutes. Serve warm, and enjoy.

Chapter 9:
Sunny Seitan-Based Recipes

Make Your Own Seitan

Recipe Makes 6 Servings.

Ingredients:

Dough Ingredients:
6 cups whole wheat flour
2 ¼ cups cold water
Broth Ingredients:
5 cups water

1 diced onion
¼ cup soy sauce
1 tbsp. miso paste
1 quartered tomatoes
3 minced garlic cloves

Directions:

Begin by mixing together the flour and the water, listed above. Mix until you've created a dough.

Next, formulate this dough into a ball, and place the dough ball in a bath of cold water. Cover the dough and allow it to sit for eight hours.

Next, knead the dough and rinse it. Squeeze the dough and remove all liquid. Slice the gluten into smaller pieces.

Next, mix the broth ingredients together in a saucepan and allow them to boil. Drop the small sliced pieces of gluten into the broth and then allow it to return to boiling immediately after. Place the heat on LOW, and then allow the broth to cook for an additional thirty minutes. At this time, remove the tomato and the onion, and toss them out.

Cover the seitan with the created broth, and store the seitan in the refrigerator. Enjoy at a later time!

Super Seitan Fajitas

Recipe Makes 4 Servings.

Ingredients:

1 pound sliced seitan
1 dice onion
1 sliced red pepper
½ tsp. chili powder

4 minced garlic cloves
½ tsp. cumin powder
2 tbsp. soy sauce
4 tbsp. olive oil

Directions:

Begin by sautéing the garlic and the onions in the olive oil for six minutes. Afterwards add all the other ingredients to the skillet and stir well for ten minutes. The seitan will become completely cooked.

Wrap the tortillas around the vegetable and seitan ingredients, and serve warm. Enjoy!

BBQ-Doused Seitan

Recipe Makes 6 Servings.

Ingredients:

1 pound sliced seitan
2 tbsp. soy sauce
3 tbsp. olive oil

3 tbsp. balsamic vinegar
3 tbsp. barbecue sauce
1 tbsp. water

Directions:

Begin by sautéing the seitan in the olive oil over medium, browning it on all sides. Next, add the vinegar, the barbecue, and the soy sauce. Administer a bit of water, and stir well.

Next, heat the seitan for two more minutes, and then serve warm with your choice of side.

Enjoy!

Seitan Slow Cooked Chow Mein

Recipe Makes 6 Servings.

Ingredients:

1 pound chopped seitan
3 diced carrots
4 chopped celery stalks
1 cup vegetable broth
5 sliced scallions
½ cup soy sauce

1 tsp. ginger
½ tsp. red pepper flakes
1/3 cup bean sprouts
8 ounces sliced water chestnuts
1/3 cup water
1/3 cup cornstarch

Directions:

Begin by bringing all the ingredients—except for the water and the cornstarch—together in a slow cooker. Cover the slow cooker and allow the mixture to cook on LOW for eight hours.

Next, stir together the water and the cornstarch, and add the mixture to the slow cooker after eight minutes. Cover the slow cooker only a little bit, and cook the mixture for an additional fifteen minutes.

Enjoy!

Dee South Seitan Fried Chicken

Recipe Makes 6 Servings.

Ingredients:

1 pound diced seitan
1 tsp. onion powder
1 tsp. black pepper
1 tsp. garlic powder
1 tsp. cayenne
1 ½ cups flour

1/3 cup nutritional yeast
2 tbsp. baking powder
1/3 cup mustard
½ cup water
olive oil

Directions:

Begin by mixing together the garlic powder, the onion powder, the salt, the flour, the pepper, the nutritional yeast, and the cayenne.

To the side, mix together the mustard and the water. Add about half of the prepared flour mix to the mustard mix, and stir well.

Next, coat the seitan with the mustard and then coat the seitan with the flour mix.

Fry these pieces of seitan in a large skillet for five minutes. Make sure to turn the seitan once or twice, and serve the "chicken" with your choice of sauce. Enjoy!

Asian-Inspired Hoisin Sauce Stir Fry

Recipe Makes 8 Servings.

Ingredients:

3 tbsp. sesame oil
4 tbsp. soy sauce
4 tbsp. Hoisin Sauce
2 tbsp. rice vinegar
1 cup vegetable broth
4 diced onions
2 cups diced broccoli

3 tbsp. sugar
1 tsp. ginger
3 minced garlic cloves
1 cup chopped seitan
1 diced bell pepper

Directions:

Begin by bringing together the sesame oil, the soy sauce, the hoisin sauce, the rice vinegar, the broth, the sugar, the ginger, the garlic, and the cornstarch in a saucepan over medium. Allow the mixture to heat for seven minutes. Afterwards, allow the mixture to cool.

Next, place the seitan and the created sauce mixture in a skillet. Allow the seitan to become lightly browned. Then, add the vegetables.

Stir well for about five minutes, and then serve your seitan stir fry. Enjoy!

Faux "Beef" Seitan Stew

Recipe makes 8 Servings.

Ingredients:

16 ounces sliced seitan
2 tbsp. olive oil
3 tbsp. soy sauce
4 tbsp. vegan butter
1 diced onion
4 diced carrots
2 diced celery stalks

3 chopped potatoes
4 minced garlic cloves
3 cups vegetable broth
3 tbsp. flour
1 tsp. brown sugar
2 tbsp. chopped thyme
salt and pepper to taste

Directions:

Begin by mixing the seitan, the soy sauce, and the olive oil together in a skillet. Next, remove the seitan and set it to the side.

Next, sauté the celery, the onions, the carrots, the potatoes, and the garlic together in the vegan butter for six minuts. Add the vegetable broth, the thyme, the flour, the sugar, the salt, and the pepper, and stir. Add the seitan, now, and simmer the stew for fifty minutes. Enjoy.

Seitan Slow Cooker Rice Pilaf

Recipe Makes 8 Servings.

Ingredients:

2 cups diced seitan
2 chopped celery stalks
1 diced carrot
1 diced onion

1/3 cup white wine
3 cups vegetable broth
2 cups rice

Directions:

Begin by bringing all the above ingredients together into the slow cooker, and cooking the ingredients on LOW for eight hours. Serve warm, and enjoy!

Vietnamese Seitan Pho

Recipe Makes 8 Servings.

Ingredients:

7 star anises

1 ½ tbsp.. coriander seeds

2 tbsp. cloves
1 tbsp. fennel seeds
1 cinnamon stick
1 sliced onion
5 sliced ginger knobs
4 cups vegetable broth
10 ounces Vietnamese rice noodles

1 tsp. soy sauce
1 cup chopped cilantro
1 cup sliced seitan
2 cups mung bean sprouts
1 cup chopped fresh basil
1 sliced scallion

Directions:

Begin by heating together the onion, the ginger, and the spices for five minutes. Next, place this mixture in a cheesecloth, and secure them together.

To the side, place the cheesecloth pack in a slow cooker. Add the soy sauce, the roth, the seitan, and the noodles. Cover the slow cooker, and cook it on low for five hours.

After four hours, remove the cheesecloth pack and serve the pho warm. Enjoy!

Friday Afternoon Seitan "BLT" Sandwich

Recipe Makes 4 Servings.

Ingredients:

8 ounces sliced seitan
1 tbsp. olive oil
1/3 cup vegan mayonnaise
4 cups sliced lettuce

1 tbsp. sliced scallions
1 tsp. lime juice
4 whole-grain sandwich rolls

Directions:

Begin by heating the olive oil in a skillet and frying the seitan until they're brown. Allow the seitan to cool. Next, blend the vegan mayo, the scallions, and the lime juice in a bowl. Spread this created aioli on the bread, and place a layer of lettuce overtop. Next, Place the seitan in the sandwich, as well, and enjoy!

Indian-Inspired Curry Seitan Kebabs

Recipe Makes 6 Servings.

Ingredients:

1 ¾ cups sliced and diced seitan
5 diced bell peppers
2 diced onions
½ cup sliced mushrooms
1 ½ cup cherry tomatoes
4 tbsp. sesame oil

½ cup olive oil
1/3 cup curry powder
2 tsp. garlic powder
1 tsp. salt
skewers

Directions:

Begin by skewering the onions, seitan, peppers, mushrooms, and tomatoes on the skewers.

To the side, mix together the olive oil, the curry powder, the sesame oil, the salt, and the garlic. Marinate the vegetables with this mixture for three hours in the refrigerator.

Next, grill the kebabs for five minutes on each side, and enjoy!

Fresh Herbed Barley and Seitan Pilaf

Recipe Makes 8 Servings.

Ingredients:

1 ½ cup diced seitan
1 ½ cup pearled barley
3 tbsp. olive oil
3 tbsp. soy sauce
4 cups vegetable broth
1 tsp. onion powder
1 cup sliced mushrooms

1 tsp. salt
1 tsp. onion powder
3 minced garlic cloves
1 tsp. cilantro
2 tsp. parsley
¼ cup diced walnuts

Directions:

Begin by sautéing the seitan with the olive oil and the soy sauce for five minutes.

To the side, place the barley and the vegetable broth in a large soup pot, and allow the mixture to simmer. Next, administer all the mushrooms, spices, and the seitan, cover the soup pot, and allow it to simmer for a full twenty-five minutes.

Next, add the walnuts and immediately remove the pot from the heat. Stir well, and enjoy!

Chicago Lover's Seitan Au Jus

Recipe Makes 1 cup.

Ingredients:

4 ounces sliced seitan
1 tbsp. olive oil
½ tsp. liquid smoke
¾ cup vegetable broth
1 minced garlic clove
1/3 cup red wine
¼ tbsp. flour
½ tbsp. vegan butter

Directions:

Begin by heating the oil ad the smoke together in a skillet for three minutes. Next, add the seitan, and cook the seitan for about six minutes.

Next, remove the seitan from the heat and add the red wine, the broth, and the garlic. Simmer the mixture for ten minutes. Afterwards, add the vegan butter and the four. Salt and pepper to serve.

Serve the au jus to the side of the seitan for extra flavorful dipping. Furthermore, utilize it to dip your seitan sandwiches in! Enjoy!

Spicy Wild West Seitan Wings

Recipe Makes 8 Servings.

Ingredients:

1 sliced pound of seitan
1 ½ tsp. onion powder
3 tsp. garlic powder

½ cup melted vegan butter
olive oil
1/3 cup hot sauce

Directions:

Begin by administering the powders to the seitan and bring it a bit in the olive oil over medium heat for eight minutes.

To the side, mix together the melted butter and the hot sauce. Coat your wings with this sauce, and serve warm. Enjoy!

New Orleans Sensation Seitan

Recipe Makes 4 Servings.

Ingredients:

4 minced garlic cloves
1 diced onion
3 cups sliced seitan
1 diced green pepper
1 tbsp. olive oil

4 tbsp. soy sauce
28 ounces diced tomatoes
2 cups diced okra
½ tsp. cayenne pepper

Directions:

Begin by sautéing the garlic, the pepper, and the onion together in olive oil for five minutes. Next, add the tomatoes, the soy sauce, and the caenne pepper.

Afterwards, add the seitan, and cover the mixture for twenty minutes. After twenty minutes, toss in the okra, and cover and cook for twelve more minutes. Serve warm over rice.

Enjoy!

Super Slow Cooked Seitan Tandoori

Recipe Makes 8 Servings.

Ingredients:

1 pound sliced seitan
1 diced onion
1/3 cup vegan yogurt
1/3 cup tomato sauce
3 minced garlic cloves

½ tsp. cayenne pepper
1 tsp. cumin
2 cloves
1 tsp. salt

Directions:

Begin by processing every ingredient—without the seitan—in a food processor to create a smooth consistency.

Next, pour this mixture into a bowl, and administer the seitan in the center. Coat the seitan with the batter.

Skewer each piece of seitan, and grill the different sides. Enjoy warm!

Norway's Seitan Stew

Recipe Makes 8 Servings.

Ingredients:

1 pound diced seitan
3 tbsp. olive oil
1 diced onion
3 minced garlic cloves
2 cups vegetable stock

1/3 cup red wine
1 tsp. chopped rosemary
1 tbsp. tamari
4 chopped carrots
1 chopped celery stalk

Directions:

Begin by bringing the olive oil, the seitan, the onion, and the garlic together in a skillet for ten minutes. Stir occasionally.

Next, pour the red wine into the pan, and completely deglaze the inside of the pan. Next, add vegetable stock, tamari, herbs, and all other vegetables.

Bring the mixture to a boil. Afterwards, cover the pot and allow it to simmer for thirty minutes. Stir every few minutes. Afterwards, serve your stew warm, and enjoy!

Dinner Date Coconut Breaded Seitan

Recipe Makes 16 nuggets.

Ingredients:

1 pound sliced seitan
1 tbsp. egg replacement
1 ¼ cup coconut milk
½ tsp. salt
5 cups coconut flakes

1 ¼ cup panko bread crumbs
1 cup all-purpose flour
1 tsp. paprika
½ cup coconut oil

Directions:

Begin by slicing the seitan into nugget-sized pieces.

To the side, mix together the egg replacement, the coconut milk, and the salt. Place the nuggets in this mixture and allow them to marinate for two hours.

Next, stir coconut flakes with panko bread crumbs, flour, paprika, and salt.

Next, pour a bit of oil in a saucepan, and dip each nugget into the coconut flour mixture in order to coat them. Fry the faux nuggets in the oil until they're golden.

Next, place the seitan on a baking sheet to cool, and enjoy when you're ready!

Mapled Seitan Sandwich

Recipe Makes 1 Sandwich.

Ingredients:

4 ounces sliced seitan
2 tsp. liquid smoke

2 tsp. mape syrup
salt and pepper to taste

Directions:

Begin by placing the seitan in a bit of olive oil. Next, add the liquid smoke and the maple to the mixture, and stir well while the seitan is cooking. Salt and pepper the seitan, and make sure the seitan is crispy.

Pile the seitan between 2 slices of multigrain bread, some vegan mayonnaise, 4 slices of avocado, and Dijon mustard. Enjoy!

Spiced Seitan Garlic Wrap

Recipe Make 4 Servings.

Ingrediens:

Recipe Makes 10 ounces of sliced seitan

½ cup rice wine vinegar

1 tbsp. sesame oil
juice from 1 lime
1 tsp. red chili flakes
1 ½ tsp. inced garli

½ tsp. Worcestershire sauce
1 tsp. grated ginger
4 large lettuce leaves

Directions:

Begin by slicing the seitan and whisking it with the other vegetable ingredients. Marinate this mixture in a large container.

To the side, heat the seitan in a skillet, and cook the seitan for five minutes.

Place the above recipe into your lettuce wrap, and roll it over itself to deliver a perfect roll. Enjoy.

Asian-Inspired Sweet and Sour Seitan

Recipe Makes 4 Servings.

Ingredients:

8 ounces sliced seitan
1 tsp. ginger paste
1 ½ tsp. minced garlic
1/3 cup white wine vinegar
1 cup orange juice

3 tbsp. agave nectar
4 tbsp. brown sugar
2 tbsp. soy sauce
3 tbsp. corn starch
¼ cup water

Directions:

Begin by placing the slices of seitan in a baking dish and baking it at 350 degrees Fahrenheit for twenty minutes.

Next, prepare the sauce. Bring the ginger and the garlic together in a skillet for two minutes. Allow the rest of the ingredients to enter—except for the seitan and the cornstarch and water.

Next, mix together the cornstarch with the water. Pour this mixture into the sauce, and stir well.

Remove the seitan from the oven, and slice it apart. Pour the created mixture overtop of the seitan, and enjoy.

Chicken-Flavored Seitan Tacos

Recipe Makes 10 Servings.

Ingredients:

2 cups ground seitan
1 diced yellow pepper

1 diced red pepper
4 tbsp. taco sauce

1 diced avocado
1 diced lime

8 corn tortilla

Directions:

Begin by dicing the vegetables, and cook these vegetables in the oil for seven minutes. Next, add the seitan and cook for an additional ten minutes. Position the above mixture, along with the non-cooked avocadoes, in each of the corn tortillas, and enjoy!

Italian Seitan with Dip

Recipe Makes 4 Servings.

Ingredients:

1 pound sliced seitan
½ cup vegan horseradish sauce
1 tbsp. safflower oil
1 cup diced onions

2 cups created seitan au jus (see other recipe)
vegan Worcestershire sauce
salt and pepper to taste.

Directions:

Begin by slicing up the seitan and placing them in a skillet with the oil. Season the seitan with Worcestershire and pepper. Cook the seitan for five minutes.

Next, place a layer of aioli on a piece of bread followed by seitan, followed by au jus juice, shown how to make in a previous recipe.

Faux Canard BBQ Pizza

Recipe Makes 8 Slices.

Ingredients:

1 store-bought pizza crust (almost always vegan, but check!)
1 cup vegan BBQ sauce
1/3 cup tomato sauce
½ cup sliced onion

1 cup sliced seitan
1 cup grated vegan mozzarella cheese
½ cup grated cheddar cheese
½ cup sliced baana peppers
½ cup pineapple chunks

Directions:

Preheat your oven to 425 degrees Fahrenheit.

Begin by mixing together half of the BBQ sauce and the tomato sauce. Spread this mixture over the pizza dough.

To the side, mix together the remaining BBQ with the seitan and allow it to sit for five minutes.

Next, sprinkle both the cheddar cheese and the mozzarella cheese over the pizza crust. Add the seitan and the rest of the vegetables over the cheese.

Bake the pizza for eleven minutes. Allow the pizza to cool for a few moments, and then enjoy warm!

Broccoli with Seitan Marinated Kabobs

Recipe Makes 10 kabobs.

Ingredients:

1 pound sliced and diced seitan
1 tbsp. tamarind
1 tbsp. soy sauce
1/3 cup agave nectar
1 tsp. ginger

½ tsp. cumin
½ tsp. salt
1 tsp. molasses
20 broccoli florets
skewers

Directions:

Begin by mixing together all of the ingredients except for the broccoli and the seitan in a small bowl.

Next, assemble the kabobs by sticking one piece of seitan followed by a piece of broccoli onto the stick. Do this until you've created 10 kabobs.

Next, place the kabobs in a bowl with the sauce, and allow the kabobs to marinate for three hours. When you're ready, grill the kabobs either on the grill or in a skillet over the stove. Allow them to get crispy and delicious, and enjoy!

Chicago-Style Smoked Seitan Brisket

Recipe Makes 8 Servings.

Ingredients:

1 pound seitan
1 diced stalk of celery
3 chopped carrots
3 cups vegetables stock
¾ cup red wine
2 tbsp. agave

1 tbsp. soy sauce
2 tsp. tomato paste
3 tbsp. canola oil
3 tbsp. all-purpose flour
½ cup vegan bbq sauce

Directions:

Begin by preheating your oven to 385 degrees Fahrenheit.

Next, place all the vegetables, the sauces, and the oil together in a large baking pan. Allow the vegetables to roast for thirty-five minutes.

Seventeen minutes into the cook time above, place the seitan in the oven in a different baking dish.

Afterwards, remove all the baking dishes and position the seitan over the cooked vegetables. Pour the red wine, the soy sauce, the stock, the agave, and the tomato paste into the mixture, and stir well. Cover the mixture with aluminum foil, and allow the mixture to roast for forty-five minutes.

Next, remove the pan, stir the ingredients, and return it to the oven for fifteen minutes.

Afterwards, remove the liquid from the baking pan, slice up the seitan, and return the seitan to the pan. Cook for ten more minutes.

Next, add the canola oil and the flour to a large pot. Cook this mixture for three minutes. Afterwards, add the created liquid from the baking seitan roast. Add a bit of soy sauce, salt, and pepper to taste. Cover this mixture and set it to the side.

Next, pour the bbq sauce over the seitan, making sure to evenly coat it. Place the seitan—by itself—on the middle rack of your oven, and set your oven to broil. Cook the seitan in the broiler for eight minutes.

Serve the seitan with the roasted vegetables, and drizzle the created gravy over the two awesome courses. Enjoy!

Inspired Chicken-Fried Seitan with Greens

Recipe Makes 4 Servings.

Ingredients:

4 cups water
2 tsp. cumin
3 tbsp. tamari

1 tsp. pepper
3 tbsp. vegan Worcestershire sauce
1 pound sliced seitan

Wet Ingredients:

1/3 cup water
4 tbsp. spicy mustard
1/3 cup oat milk
1 tsp. garlic powder
3 tbsp. flour
1 tbsp. nutritional yeast
1 tsp. cumin
Dry ingredients:
1 tsp. salt
1 1/3 cup flour
1 tsp. cumin

4 tbsp. nutritional yeast
2 tsp. paprika

Directions:

Begin by preparing the broth by mixing together the water, the cumin, the tamari, the pepper, and the Worcestershire sauce in a saucepan. Allow the mixture to simmer for ten minutes, and then remove it from the heat.

Next, mix together all the wet ingredients in one bowl and all the dry ingredients in another.

Heat a pot of canola oil to three hundred and fifty degrees Fahrenheit.

Next, dip a slice of seitan in the dry mix followed by the wet mix. Then, dip it one last time in the dry mix, and fry the seitan tender for a few minutes on each side until it becomes golden.

Serve the tender with a side of gravy and some roasted broccoli, and enjoy!

Living the High Life Seitan Steaks

Recipe Makes 4 Steaks.

3 Ingredients:

4 seitan steaks
1 tsp. curry powder
1 tsp.pepper
1 tbsp. vegan butter

½ cup almond milk
4 large baked potatoes
½ tsp. nutmeg

Directions:

Begin by slicing and dicing the baked potatoes. Mash the potatoes and add the soy milk and the butter to them. Stir well.

Next, heat a bit of canola or olive oil in a skillet and fry the steaks for about six minutes on each side. Next, pepper and curry and nutmeg the steak and cook for one additional minute on each side.

Enjoy your "meat and potatoes" dinner!

Warm Evening Seitan Beef Stew

Recipe Makes 8 Servings.

Ingredients:

1 diced onion
2 tbsp. olive oil
4 minced garlic cloves
3 chopped carrots
1 tsp. rosemary

2 cups red wine
1 tsp. paprika
1 tsp. thyme
1 tsp. crushed fennel
2 ounces sliced mushrooms

4 cups vegetable broth
2 pounds sliced and diced potatoes
1/3 cup all-purpose flour

¾ cup water
3 tbsp. tomato paste

Directions:

Begin by bringing all of the above ingredients together in a slow cooker, and heating the slow cooker to LOW. Cook the mixture for eight hours on this low temperature, stirring every few hours. Enjoy!

Vibrant Colored Quinoa and Seitan Salad

Recipe Makes 4 Servings.

Ingredients:

2 cups cubed seitan
1 cup peas
3 diced carrots
2 cups cooked quinoa
½ cup soaked almonds

3 tbsp. soy sauce
1 diced red bell pepper
1 tbsp. brown rice vinegar
2 tbsp. sesame oil
1 cup water

Directions:

Begin by bringing the chopped carrots and the peas together in a bowl along with the cooked seitan and the quinoa. Stir well.

Next, bring together the last six ingredients in a blender or food processor to create the sauce. Pulse well, and pour this mixture over the created seitan mixture. Stir well, and enjoy!

Eggplant Agenda Seitan Stew

Recipe Makes 8 Servings.

Ingredients:

1 diced onion
1 ½ cup split peas
3 sliced red chile peppers
5 cups water
2 tsp. salt
1 diced eggplant
3 tbsp. molasses
2 cups sliced seitan
1 tsp. paprika
¼ tsp. cinnamon
¼ tsp. nutmeg

1 tsp. cumin
salt and pepper to taste

Directions:

Bring all the ingredients above into a slow cooker and cook the stew on LOW for eight hours. Stir every few hours, and serve warm. Enjoy!

Seitan at the Summertime Deli Sandwich

Recipe Makes 1 sandwich.

Ingredients:

2 slices seitan
2 pieces whole-wheat bread
vegan mayonnaise

3 slices onion
1 slice tomato
2 slices dill pickles

Directions:

Assemble the above sandwich by first allowing the seitan to be heated in olive oil in a skillet.

Next, position the seitan pieces, the vegan mayonnaise, the onion, the tomato, and the dill pickle in the two slices of whole-wheat bread, and enjoy your deli-inspired sandwich!

Thanksgiving Dinner Seitan "Turkey"

Recipe Makes 1 "turkey."

Ingredients:

2 ¼ cup wheat gluten
1/3 cup soy sauce
1 cup vegan "chicken" broth
3 tbsp. olive oil
3 tbsp. agave nectar
1/8 tsp. liquid smoke

1/3 cup nutritional yeast flakes
14 ounces firm tofu
2 tsp. poultry seasoning
1 tsp. onion powder
1 tsp. garlic powder
¼ tsp. turmeric

Directions:

Begin by mixing together all the wet ingredients, the tofu, the nutritional yeast, and the spices except for the wheat gluten in a blender until completely smooth.

Next, add the mixed ingredients together with the wheat gluten, and mix the ingredients well. Knead the ingredients with your hands, and roll the mixture into a loaf-like shape.

Wrap aluminum foil around the seitan log, and place the log in a pot with water. Place a can of beans beneath the seitan log to keep it "up" in the water.

Next, allow the seitan to steam for one hour. Next, allow it to cool, and slice the seitan for your turkey meal.

Enjoy!

Cilantro and Lime Seitan Munch

Recipe Makes 4 Servings.

Ingredients:

3 tbsp. olive oil
1 sliced jalapeno
1 diced onion
10 ounces sliced seitan
1/3 cup chopped cilantro

1 cup corn
10 ounces sliced mushrooms
4 minced garlic cloves
4 tbsp. lime juice
salt and pepper to taste

Directions:

Begin by preheating a large pan at medium heat. Add two tsp. of olive oil, garlic cloves, jalapeno peppers, and onions to the oil, and then cook the mixture for six minutes.

Next, add the corn and the seitan to the skillet, and add one more tbsp.. of oil. Cook for an additional seven minutes.

Next, add the cilantro, the mushrooms, and the salt and pepper to taste. Cook for six more minutes.

Add the lime and stir well. Serve warm, and enjoy!

Taco Tuesday Spicy Seitan

Recipe Makes 8 tacos.

Ingredients:

16 corn tortillas
1 cup vegan carrot coleslaw
2 cup sliced teriyaki seitan

1 cup sliced onions
1 cup chopped cilantro

Directions:

Begin by warming the tortillas on a skillet. Place the tortillas to the side, and then heat up the seitan in the skillet for about three minutes on each side.

Place a layer of the seitan in the taco followed by the coleslaw, the onions, and the cilantro. Add any sauce, if you please, and enjoy!

Festival Occasion Teriyaki Seitan

Recipe Makes 1 pound seitan.

Ingredients:

1 cup vital wheat gluten
1 tsp. paprika
1/3 cup whole-wheat flour
1 tsp. onion powder
2 tbsp. soy sauce

½ cup water
½ tsp. liquid smoke
2 tbsp. vegan Worcestershire sauce
3 tbsp. vegetable oil
1 cup Teriyaki sauce

Directions:

Begin by mixing together the dry ingredients. To the side, mix together the wet ingredients. Bring the two mixtures together, and stir well to create a dough. Cover the dough and allow it to sit for thirty minutes.

Next, preheat the oven to 350 degrees Fahrenheit. Create a log-like shape with the dough, and place it on a baking sheet, covered with aluminum foil. Allow the log to bake for one hour. Afterwards, allow the seitan to cool, and slice it into strips. Enjoy with the teriyaki glaze.

Asian-Inspired Seitan Rolls

Recipe Makes 8 Servings.

Ingredients:

3 cups sliced and diced seitan
½ cup hoisin sauce
4 tbsp. water
1/3 cup mirin
3 tsp. Sriracha

1 tsp. sesame oil
1 tsp. minced ginger
3 bunched sliced scallions
2 tbsp. toasted sesame seeds
toothpicks

Directions:

Begin by creating the marinade by mixing together all the ingredients except for the seitan in a bowl. Slice the seitan, and place the slices in the created marinade for two hours.

Next, add the scallions to the bowl, making sure that the seitan and the scallions are separated in the bowl.

Form the rolls by places a slice of seitan on a dinner plate. Follow the seitan with five scallions over the slice. Next, roll up the seitan around the vegetables, and secure the seitan with a toothpick.

Next, heat the skillet over medium and cook the created seitan rolls for about three minutes on each side. Serve the rolls warm with a little extra Sriracha and some sesame seeds. Enjoy!

Vietnamese-Inspired Faux Duck Sandwich

Recipe Makes 4 Sandwiches.

Directions:

1 cup julienned radishes
3 tbsp. sugar
1 cup julienned carrots
1/3 cup white vinegar
½ tsp. salt
¾ cup water

4 Vietnamese sandwich rolls
½ pound sliced seitan
1 tsp. curry powder
1 sliced cucumber
1 cup chopped cilantro
vegan mayonnaise to taste

Directions:

Begin by stirring together the sugar, the salt, the vinegar, the water, the radishes, and the carrots. Cover this mixture and chill it for two hours.

Afterwards, add the curry to the seitan, and sauté the seitan in some olive oil for about five minutes on each side.

Next, toast the vegan bread, and spread the bread with mayonnaise and all the other remaining toppings, including the chilled topping. Fold the sandwich up, and enjoy!

Gotta Love It Seitan Piccada

Recipe Makes 8 Servings.

Ingredients:

1 pound sliced seitan
½ cup flour
olive oil
5 minced garlic cloves
1/3 cup white wine

3 cups vegetable broth
salt and pepper to taste
1/3 cup capers
3 tbsp. lemon juice
3 tbsp. nutritional yeast flakes

Directions:

Begin by preheating the skillet and then coating the seitan slices in flour. Pour a bit of olive oil in the skillet, and cook the seitan until it's browned. Place the seitan on a covered plate in order to keep it warm.

Next, make the sauce with the rest of the ingredients, pouring everything into the skillet and stirring the ingredients well. Pull the sauce into a rolling boil, and allow the mixture to boil for eight minutes.

Next, serve the seitan with the prepared sauce overtop, and enjoy!

Middle Eastern Seitan Shawarma

Recipe Makes 4 Servings.

Ingredients:

1 pound seitan
½ cup boiling water
3 tsp. nutritional yeast
1 diced onion
3 tbsp. lemon juice

2 tbsp. vinegar
2 tsp. Dijon mustard
½ tsp. cumin
½ tsp. ginger
salt and pepper to taste

Directions:

Begin by slicing the seitan.

Next, pour the nutritional yeast into a pan of boilng water. Add the rest of the ingredients, and stir well. Mix this created sauce with the seitan strips, and allow the seitan to marinate for two hours. Afterwards, fry the seitan strips on each side for five minutes, and serve warm.

Seitan Alice Pineapple Rice

Recipe Makes 8 Servings.

Ingredients:

½ cup olive oil
1/3 cup pineapple juice
3 tsp. sesame oil
2 minced garlic cloves
1 cup chunked pineapple
½ tsp. red pepper flakes
2 tsp. ginger
½ tsp. sea salt

2 cups packed arugula
3 cups cooked brown rice
5 sliced onions
1 cup chopped cashews
3 sliced shallots
1 minced chili
6 ounces sliced and diced seitan

Directions:

Begin by mixing together the first eight ingredients—the sauce—and blending it in a food processor. Simmer the ingredients for about five minutes a few minutes before serving.

Next, toss the arugula with the created dressing.

Next, bring together the brown rice, the onions, the cashews, the shallots, and the chili. Toss this mixture with the arugula and the sauce.

Next, fry the seitan in the skillet for about three minutes on each side, and portion the seitan out with the rest of the rice mixture. Enjoy!

Ancient Orange Vegan Seitan

Recipe Makes 4 Servings.

Ingredients:

½ pound sliced seitan
1 cup orange juice
2 tbsp. agave
2 tbsp. liquid aminos

2 minced garlic cloves
1 tsp. minced ginger
1 tsp. cornstarch
salt and pepper to taste

Directions:

Begin by mixing together all the ingredients except for the seitan in a large bowl. Place the seitan in the bowl, and allow the seitan to marinate for three hours.

Next, fry the seitan in an oiled skillet for four minutes on each side, and enjoy with a side of rice.

Seitan Mixed with Polenta

Recipe Makes 4 Servings.

Ingredients:

20 ounces tube polenta
2 tbsp. olive oil
1 pound sliced seitan
2 tbsp. soy sauce
7 sliced stalks of bok choy

8 ounces spinach
5 sliced scallions
½ cup sliced sun-dried tomatoes
2 tbsp. balsamic vinegar
salt and pepper to taste

Directions:

Begin by slicing the polenta into pieces with half-inch thickness. Next, heat a skillet, and add the oil to the skillet to create a nice coating. Add the polenta and cook it for five minutes on each side.

Next, place the polenta on a side plate, and heat the soy sauce in the skillet. Add the seitan and stir. Allow the seitan to sauté for five minutes. Next, add the spinach, the bok choy, and the scallions, and cover the mixture to allow the greens to wilt.

Add the vinegar, the sun-dried tomatoes, and the polenta, next, and serve with salt and pepper. Enjoy!

Coconut Spinach Seitan Sloppy Joes

Recipe Makes 6 Sandiwhces.

Ingredients:

1 tbsp. coconut oil
1 diced oinion
1 sliced and diced pound of seitan
4 inced garlic cloves
1 tbsp. paprika
2 tbsp. thyme
½ tsp. crushed red pepper flakes
½ tsp. allspice
14 ounces crushed tomatoes
¼ tsp. cinnamon

3 tbsp. maple syrup
1 tbsp. lime juice
2 tsp. yellow mustard
Spinach Ingredients:
3 tsp. coconut oil
1 pound de-stemmed spinach
3 minced garlic cloves
1 ½ cup coconut milk
3 star anise

Directions:

Begin by preparing the sloppy joe mixture by sautéing the onion in coconut oil for five minutes. Next, toss the seitan in the mix and continue to cook for ten minutes. Push this mixture to the side of the skillet to create the ginger and garlic sauté. Stir well, and add the additional spices, the tomatoes, the maple syrup, the mustard, and the lime juice. Stir well, cooking for about ten more minutes.

Next, make the spinach by sautéing the garlic, the spinach, and the coconut oil together. Next, try to drain all the excess water from the pan into the sink. Add the coconut milk, the star anise, and any salt you might like, and allow this mixture to boil. Let the spinach sit off the heat for ten minutes.

Next, assemble the sandwiches by placing a bit of the sloppy joe mix in a bun topped with the spinach mixture. Enjoy!

Lemoned Seitan

Recipe Makes 4 Servings.

Ingredients:

½ pound sliced seitan
2 sliced lemons
4 minced garlic cloves
10 pitted green olives

4 tbsp. white wine
1 ½ cups vegetable broth
2 tbsp. minced parsley
salt and pepper to taste

Directions:

Begin by placing the lemon slices and the garlic in a skillet. Cook the slices for about three minutes. Afterwards, remove the lemon and leave the garlic. Add the green olives, the vegetable broth, the lemon juice, and the wine, and allow the mixture to cook for a bout four minutes. Next, place the seitan in the skillet to assimilate with the ingredients. Coat the seitan with the sauce, and cook each side for about five minutes.

Garnish the seitan with lemon, and enjoy!

Spiced Seitan Curry

Recipe Makes 4 Servings.

Ingredients:

1 diced onion
1-inch minced ginger piece
4 minced garlic cloves
2 diced peppers
2 ½ cups diced seitan pieces
1 tsp. coriander
1 tsp. cumin

1 tbsp. curry powder
½ tsp. cardamom
1 chopped and peeled mango
1 can coconut milk
1 sliced zucchini
1 sliced carrot
1 sliced squash

Directions:

Begin by sautéing together the garlic, the peppers, the ginger, and the onions in the olive oil for three minutes. Next, add the seitan and all the spices, and stir for five minutes. Next, add the mango, the coconut milk, the carrots, and the squash. Stir continuously for three minutes. Next, cover the mixture, and allow it to simmer for ten minutes. Enjoy over rice.

Seitan Roulade Made with a Vegan Stuffing

Recipe Makes 8 Servings.

Ingredients:

3 cups sliced seitan
3 tbsp. olive oil
10 sliced mushrooms
3 sliced shallots
8 chopped sage leaves

1 1/3 cups chopped chestnuts
5 cups cubed vegan bread
1 cup vegetable broth
1 tbsp. chopped marjoram

Directions:

Begin by heating the shallots and the oil together in a skillet. Add the carrots and the mushrooms, next, along with the chestnuts and the herbs. Stir twice, and then toss in the bread. Pour the broth into the mixture a bit at a time and season the stuffing with salt and pepper.

Portion the created stuffing onto the strips of seitan, and roll the seitan up, sealing it with a toothpick. In a different skillet, place the seitan rolls on oiled heat, and cook both sides. Enjoy the seitan and stuffing wraps.

Chapter 10:
Tofu-Based Dinner Recipes

Make-At-Home Tofu

Recipe Makes 1 pound tofu.

Ingredients:

1 pound uncooked soybeans
4 tsp. magnesium chloride

Directions:

Begin by making sure you have a tofu mold: a rectangle of 8 inches by 6 inches to place the tofu in for it to solidify.

Next, create the soybean milk by soaking soybeans overnight. Place one cup of soybeans to three cups of water in the blender, and blend well. Do this for all of the soybeans. Next, heat the soybean milk for ten minutes, and strain it into a large bowl. This is your soybean milk.

Next, heat this soybean milk to around 200 degrees Fahrenheit. After it reaches this temperature, add the magnesium sulfate, and stir well. The milk will become thick. Place the tofu mold in your sink and place a cheesecloth in the mold. Pour the created tofu into the mold, and fold the cheesecloth over the tofu in the mold. Place a heavy, flat surface over the cheeseclothed tofu, and allow the tofu to sit for twenty minutes. Afterwards, allow the tofu to be stored in water in the fridge for 10 days. Enjoy.

Peanut Sauce Tofu Sandwiches

Recipe Makes 3 sandwiches.

Ingredients:

14 ounces firm tofu
1 tbsp. peanut oil
7 tbsp. peanut butter
1 tbsp. soy sauce
3 tbsp. rice vinegar
2 tbsp. ginger juice

3 tsp. brown sugar
1 tbsp. coconut milk
4 sandwich tortillas
1 shredded carrot
1 sliced red pepper
lime wedges

Directions:

Begin by crisping the tofu in a skillet with the peanut oil for five minutes on each side.

Next, stir together the peanut butter, the soy sauce, the rice vinegar, the ginger juice, the coconut milk, and the brown sugar.

Fold the tofu, the carrots, the peppers, the lime wedges, and the created sauce into the tortilla, and enjoy.

Tofu Tundra Scramble

Recipe Makes 6 Servings.

Ingredients:

14 ounces tofu
1 tsp. turmeric
2 tsp. garlic powder
1 ½ tbsp. nutritional yeast
1 tbsp. olive oil

5 ounces sliced mushrooms
4 cups chopped spinach
1 diced onion
6 whole-wheat tortillas

Directions:

Begin by stirring together the garlic powder, the nutritional yeast, the turmeric, the tofu, and the nutritional yeast. Set this to the side.

Next, heat the olive oil in a skillet with the onion, the mushrooms, the spinach, and the tofu. Cook and stir for five minutes.

Next, place this mixture into a tortilla and fold the tortilla into a sandwich. Enjoy!

Noodle Tofu Salad

Recipe Makes 5 Servings.

Ingredients:

3 minced garlic cloves
2 diced onions
3 tbsp. brown sugar
½ cup soy sauce
½ cup rice vinegar
2 tbsp. lime juice
1 tsp. red pepper flakes

15 ounces firm tofu
4 ounces cooked rice noodles
3 sliced carrots
1 tbsp. sesame oil
1 ½ sliced cucumber
1/3 cup chopped basil

Directions:

Begin by bringing all the first seven ingredients together in a small bowl.

Next, bring half of the prepared dressing and the tofu together in a bag. Toss the bag around and coat the tofu. Allow it to sit for thirty minutes.

Next, heat the oil in a skillet and cook the tofu until it's golden brown. Remove the tofu from the heat.

Next, place the noodles, the tofu, the basil, and the carrots together in a bowl. Top the bowl with the sauce and enjoy!

Asparagus and Tofu Red Curry

Recipe Makes 4 Servings.

Ingredients:

1 ½ tbsp.. olive oil
14 ounces tofu
1 cup vegetable broth
1/3 cup red curry paste
1 can coconut milk

2 tbsp. brown sugar
1 tsp. soy sauce
1 sliced red pepper
¾ pound diced asparagus

Directions:

Begin by heating the oil in a skillet and adding the tofu to the oil, cooking it on all sides for five minutes. Next, flip the tofu and continue to cook.

Remove the tofu from the skillet, and add the coconut milk to the skillet, cooking on medium-high. Allow it to thicken before adding the red curry paste and cooking for an additional minute.

Next, add the broth, the sugar, and the soy sauce. As this sauce begins to simmer, add the red pepper and cook for three additional minutes. Add the asparagus and continue to cook for five minutes. Position the tofu back in the skillet and coat the tofu with the created sauce. Remove the sauce from the heat and serve warm over your rice or noodle of choice. Enjoy!

BBQ Blast Off Tofu

Recipe Makes 4 Servings.

Ingredients:

14 ounces tofu
1/3 cup barbecue sauce
oil

Directions:

Begin by pressing the tofu and slicing and dicing it.

Next, pour the barbecue sauce into a baking dish, and place the tofu in the dish after it. Coat the tofu, and allow the tofu to marinate for one hour.

Next, preheat the oven to 400 degrees Fahrenheit, and oil the bottom of a baking sheet. Position the tofu bites on the baking sheet and allow the tofu to bake for twenty-five minutes. Pour more barbecue over the tofu, and bake the tofu for twenty more minutes. Enjoy with additional barbecue, if you so please.

Tropical Coconut Tofu Soup

Recipe Makes 4 Servings.

Ingredients:

4 cups vegetable broth
13 ounces coconut milk
2-inch diced ginger piece
10 ounces sliced mushrooms
14 ounces tofu

5 tbsp. lime juice
4 tbsp. soy sauce
3 tsp. brown sugar
1 sliced jalapeno pepper
1 cup chopped cilantro

Directions:

Begin by mixing together the ginger and the broth in a soup pot and allowin it to boil over high. Next, reduce the heat and bring it to a simmer for fifteen minutes.

Next, add the coconut milk, the tofu, the mushrooms, the lime juice, the soy sauce, the brown sugar, the jalapeno, and half of the cilantro leaves, and stir for about five more minutes, allowing it to simmer once more.

Serve warm, and add additional cilantro overtop. Enjoy!

Indian-style Curry Vindaloo with Tofu

Recipe make 6 servings.

Ingredients:

3 tbsp. vegetable oil
1 cup vegetable broth
½ head cauliflower
2 in. piece of ginger root
3 carrots
2 onions

1 cup mushrooms
1 can chickpeas, drained and rinsed
6 tbsp. tomato paste
3 tbsp. vindaloo-style curry power
16 fl. oz. coconut milk
1 lb extra-firm tofu

Directions:

Prepare your vegetables by peeling and slicing the carrots, halving and slicing the onions, slicing the mushooms, and cutting the cauliflower into florets. Peel and mince the ginger root. Drain the can of chickpeas and rinse them. Cut the tofu into approximately 1 inch squares.

In a large pot on medium heat, heat up the vegetable oil. Next, add the ginger root and cook until browned. The vegetables go in next! Cook until softened, stirring frequently.

Add in the tomato paste and stir until it is of a smooth consistency. Once that is done, stir in the curry powder, coconut milk, vegetable broth, tofu, mushrooms, and chickpeas. Cover the pot and simmer the concoction for at least 15 minutes, stirring infrequently.

Enjoy!

Sizzlin' BBQ Tofu Burgers

Recipe makes six servings.
Ingredients:
3 tbsp. vegetable oil
1 onion
12 oz. extra-firm tofu
2 cups vegan barbecue sauce (dealer's choice)
6 whole-wheat hamburger buns

Directions:

Begin by draining and slicing the tofu into slices half an inch thick. Slice the onion.

Heat the vegetable oil in a skillet. Add the tofu and fry until the strips are brown. Flip the strips, making sure they are golden on each side. Add the onion slices and cook to your personal preference. Slather on the barbecue sauce and turn the heat down to low. The barbecue tofu will be ready 10-15 minutes later.

Serve on the whole-wheat hamburger buns and enjoy!

Indian-Inspired Tofu Garam Masala

Recipe makes four servings.

Ingredients:

½ cup vegan yogurt
3 Serrano peppers
4 garlic cloves
1 head cauliflower
1 cup frozen peas
16 oz. tomato sauce
¼ cup cilantro

3 tsp. garam masala
4 tsp. cumin
2 tsp. fresh lemon juice
4 tsp. coriander
1 tsp. paprika
2 cups vegan cream
2 tbsp. vegan butter

Directions:

Refer to the earlier recipes for the vegan yogurt, vegan cream, and vegan butter.

Begin by preheating the oven to 375 degrees.

Drain and slice the tofu into half inch-sized cubes. Create a mixture of the vegan yogurt, the paprika, the lemon juice, two teaspoons of the cumin, and 1 teaspoon of the garam masala. Add the tofu cubes to the mixture and stir. Remove the tofu cubes and arrange on a greased baking sheet. Insert the sheet into the oven and bake for 45 minutes, rotating the tofu slices every 15 minutes.

While the tofu is baking, mince the garlic cloves and Serrano peppers. Cut the cauliflower into florets. Cook the garlic and peppers together over medium heat with the vegan butter in a skillet until softened. Then add in the rest of the cumin, garam masala, and the coriander. After a minute, add the tomato sauce and cauliflower. Cover the skillet and let it cook for 15 minutes. Stir frequently.

Once this is done, stir in the baked tofu cubes from earlier. Also add the vegan cream and frozen peas. Simmer for about five minutes.

Enjoy!

Italian Tofu Lasagna

Recipe Makes 8 Servings.

Ingredients:

12 ounces uncooked lasagna noodles
2 tbsp. soymilk
12 ounces crumbled tofu
1 cup tomato sauce
2 egg replacements

2 cups shredded vegan mozzarella
½ cup shredded vegan Parmesan
½ tsp. nutmeg
salt and pepper to taste

Directions:

Begin by preheating the oven to 350 degrees Fahrenheit.

Next, allow the lasagna noodles to boil for fifteen minutes in a pot of water.

To the side, mix together the egg replacements, the tofu, the salt, the pepper, the nutmeg, the soymilk, the tomato sauce, and a cup of shredded vegan mozzarella. Spread this mixture into the bottom of the 9x13 baking pan.

Next, place a layer of the lasagna noodles overtop followed by the sauce. Layer this mixture as many times as you can until you run out of ingredients, and top the lasagna with vegan cheese.

Next, bake the lasagna for thirty-five minutes, and serve warm. Enjoy!

Divine Tofu-Based Hummus

Recipe Makes 8 Servings.

Ingredients:

¾ cup diced tofu
2 tbsp. olive oil
1/3 cup lemon juice

2 ½ tbsp. peanut butter
15 ounces garbanzo beans
4 garlic cloves

Directions:

Begin by bringing all the above ingredients together in a food processor or blender. Blend the mixture to reach your desired hummus consistency, and chill the hummus. Serve with vegetables, and enjoy!

African-Inspired Tofu Dinner

Recipe Makes 5 Servings.

Ingredients:

3 minced garlic cloves
1 cup white rice
2 ½ cups water
1 cubed pound of tofu
4 tbsp. peanut oil

3 minced garlic cloves
6 ounces tomato paste
1/3 cup peanut butter
1 diced onion

Directions:

Begin by boiling the water and the rice together in a large pot. Cover the pot and allow the rice to simmer for twenty minutes.

Next, heat the oil in a skillet over medium heat, and brown the tofu in the skillet for ten minutes. Next, toss in the garlic and the onion, and stir and cook for six minutes. Add the peanut butter and the tomato paste, and stir the mixture for five minutes. Serve this mixture over the already cooked rice, and enjoy.

Indian-Inspired Tofu Keema

Recipe Makes 4 Servings.

Ingredients:

16 ounces firm tofu
1 cup thawed peas
1 tsp. cumin
4 tbsp. olive oil
2 tsp. curry powder

1 ½ cup chopped tomatoes
1 diced onion
1 ½ tsp. minced ginger
2 tsp. minced ginger
2 minced jalapeno peppers

Directions:

Begin by mincing the tofu and setting it to the side.

Next, heat the oil, the cumin, the onion, the ginger, and the garlic together in a skillet. After five minutes, add the peas, the tofu, and the curry powder. Continue to stir.

Next, add the tomatoes and salt and pepper the mixture. Cover the pot, and allow the mixture to simmer for twenty minutes. Lastly, add the jalapeno peppers, and cook for three more minutes before serving. Enjoy!

Chinese Braised Tofu

Recipe Makes 4 Servings.

Ingredients:

14 ounces tofu
4 ounces sliced mushrooms
3 tbsp. sesame oil
2 cups snow peas

1 tsp. soy sauce
10 ounces water chestnuts
1 cup water

Directions:

Begin by slicing up the tofu.

Fry the tofu in the sesame oil in a skillet. Fry them for five minutes on each side.

Next, slice the tofu into smaller cubes and place them to the side. Add the water chestnuts, the snow peas, and the mushrooms to the skillet, and stir well. Next, add the soy sauce to the skillet and the already cooked tofu. Cover the skillet and allow the mixture to cook on low for fifteen minutes prior to serving warm. Enjoy!

Vegan Stroganoff

Recipe Makes 8 Servings.

Ingredients:

16 ounces spaghetti noodles
24 ounces tofu
3 tbsp. vegan sour cream
1 tbsp. olive oil
3 diced onion

12 ounces coconut milk (without the liquid)
8 ounces sliced mushrooms
2 tbsp. soy sauce
2 tsp. minced garlic

Directions:

Begin by allowing the spaghetti noodles to boil in a pot of water. Cook the noodles for ten minutes.

Afterwards, drain the pot.

Heat the olive oil in a skillet on medium, and then sauté the tofu for ten minutes, stirring all the time. Set this mixture on a side plate.

Next, place the onions, the mushrooms, the garlic, and the soy sauce in the skillet and heat them together for seven minutes.

To the side, mix together the coconut milk—without the water, just the cream—and the vegan sour cream. Stir well, and add this mixture to the skillet. Add the tofu to the skillet and cook for five more minutes. Pour this mixture over the spaghetti noodles, and enjoy!

Samurai Tofu Salad

Recipe Makes 4 Servings.

Ingredients:

14 ounces tofu
1 tbsp. rice wine
4 tbsp. soy sauce
3 tsp. sesame oil
2 tbsp. olive oil
1/3 cup chopped cilantro
2 tbsp. sesame seeds

1 tbsp. rice vinegar
1 chopped tomato
1 tsp. diced ginger
1 sliced onion

Directions:

Begin by stirring together the rice wine, the soy sauce, the sesame oil, and the rice vinegar in a medium-sized bowl.

Next, heat up this mixture in a skillet and add the ginger and the garlic. Cook for five minutes.

Next, slice and dice the tofu, and place the tofu in the skillet with onion, tomato, and cilantro. Add the sesame seeds at the last minute, and stir well prior to serving. Enjoy!

Cauliflower-Based Tofu Masala

Recipe Makes 4 Servings.

Ingredients:

16 ounces tofu
4 minced serrano peppers
1/3 cup vegan yogurt
1 tsp. cayenne pepper
3 tbsp. lemon juice
2 tsp. cumin
3 tsp. coriander

2 tsp. garam masala
1 cubed cauliflower
1 tbsp. ginger root
2 cups coconut milk
1/3 cup diced cilantro
2 tbsp. vegan butter
5 minced garlic cloves

Directions:

Begin by preheating the oven to 375 degrees Fahrenheit.

Next, stir together the vegan yogurt, the cumin, the lemon juice, the cayenne, the ginger, and the salt and pepper. Slice and dice the tofu, and stir the tofu in with the created mixture. Next, place the tofu on a baking sheet and bake the tofu for one hour.

To the side, melt the vegan butter in a skillet with the garlic and the Serrano peppers for three minutes. Next, add the coriander and the garam masala. Next add the tomato sauce and the cauliflower pieces. Cover the mixture and allow the mixture to simmer for twenty minutes.

After the cauliflower has cooked all the way through, add the coconut milk, the cilantro, and the tofu mixture. Cook this complete mixture for seven minutes on medium, and serve warm. Enjoy.

Tofu "Meatloaf"

Recipe Makes 12 Servings.

Ingredients:

14 ounces tofu
1 cup panko bread crumbs
2 pounds ground seitan
1/3 cup minced bell pepper
1 ounce dry onion soup mix

1/3 cup soy sauce
1/3 cup brown sugar
2 egg replacements
1 tsp. yellow mustard

Directions:

Begin by preheating the oven to 350 degrees Fahrenehit.

Next, mix together the seitan, the tofu, the panko crumbs, the green pepper, the soup mix, and the egg replacements. Bring this mixture into the bread pan, and mold it into a flat creation. Add the rest of the ingredients to the top: the brown sugar, the soy sauce, and the mustard.

Bake the created meatloaf for forty-five minutes, and serve warm. Enjoy!

Tofu-Based Split Pea Soup

Recipe Makes 8 Servings.

Ingredients:

1 diced onion
1 tbsp. olive oil
4 minced garlic cloves
5 cups vegetable broth
1 diced carrot
5 diced red potatoes
¾ pound green split peas

8 ounces chopped spinach
16 ounces tofu
½ tbsp. basil
salt and pepper to taste

Directions:

Begin by placing the oil in a skillet and sautéing the onion and the garlic together for five minutes.

Bring all the above ingredients together in a slow cooker and cook the soup for eight hours on LOW. After eight hours, blend the soup in a blender or a food processor, and serve the soup warm.

Enjoy!

Chapter 11:
Bean and Lentil Based Dinner Recipes

Flaxseed and Quinoa Crisp Gluten Cakes

Recipe Makes 12 quinoa cakes.

Ingredients:

2 cups cooked quinoa
1 cup chopped kale
2 tbsp. ground flax
6 tbsp. water
½ cup grated sweet potato
1/3 cup ground oats
1/3 cup sunflower seeds

1/3 cup chopped sun-dried tomatoes
1 minced garlic clove
3 tbsp. diced onion
1/3 cup chopped basil
2 tsp. red wine vinegar
1 tsp. salt
4 tbsp. flour

Directions:

Begin by preheating the oven to 400 degrees Fahrenheit.

Next, mix together the flax and the water together in a small bowl. Set this together to the side for five minutes.

Next, combine all the above ingredients together in a large bowl, including the cooked quinoa. Stir well, and shape the mixture into the hamburger-like patties.

Next, bake the patties for fifteen minutes on a baking sheet. Flip the patties, and bake them for another ten minutes.

Cool the hamburger patties, and enjoy!

Lentil-Based Taco Meat

Recipe Makes Meat for 8 Tacos.

Ingredients:

1 1/3 cup green lentils
2 tsp. oregano
1 ½ cup toasted walnut pieces
1 ½ tsp. chili powder

1 ½ tsp. cumin
1 ½ tbsp. olive oil
3 tbsp. water

Directions:

Begin by cooking the lentils in a pot of water. Bring the water to a boil, and then allow the lentils to simmer for twenty-five minutes.

Next, toast the walnuts in a 300 degree oven on a baking sheet for fifteen minutes. Set the walnuts to the side to allow them to cool.

Next, mix together the walnuts and the lentils along with the spices and a bit of water to create your taco meat. Fill the meat into your favorite corn tortillas, and enjoy with your choice of topping. Enjoy!

Lentil Cranberry Meatballs

Recipe Makes 14 balls.

Ingredients:

1 cup diced walnuts
½ cup green lentils
3 minced garlic cloves
2 cups chopped mushrooms
½ cups craisins
½ tsp. oregano
½ tsp. thyme

½ cup ground oats
2 tbsp. ground flax
3 tbsp. water
1 tbsp. vinegar
1 cup chopped kale
1 tsp. salt

Directions:

Begin by cooking the lentils together in a saucepan with 3 cups of water. Allow the water to boil. Afterwards, allow the lentils to simmer for twenty minutes.

To the side, preheat the oven to 325 degrees Fahrenheit. Next, toast the walnuts in the oven for fifteen minutes. Afterwards, increase the oven temperature to 350 degrees Fahrenheit.

Next, pour the oil into a skillet with the garlic and the mushrooms. Saute the mixture for ten minutes. Afterwards, add the kale, the cranberries, the walnuts, the vinegar, and the herbs. Stir well for four minutes, and then remove the mixture from the heat.

Next, stir together the water and the flax, and then pour the mixture into the skillet. Add the oat flour, and salt and pepper the mixture.

After you're done stirring, you should have a sticky consistency. Create small balls from the lentil mixture and place them on a baking sheet. Bake the balls for fifteen minutes. Afterwards, remove the baking sheet, flip the meatballs, and cook them for another fifteen.

Allow the meatballs to cool for a few minutes before serving them. Enjoy.

Chickpea Sweet Potato Burgers

Recipe Makes 8 Patties.

Ingredients:

1 grated sweet potato
1/3 cup chopped basil
1/3 cup chopped cilantro

3 tsp. ginger
4 minced garlic cloves
1 cup processed oats

2 tbsp. ground flax
3 tbsp. water
15 ounces chickpeas

1 tsp. lime juice
1 ½ tsp. coriander
1 tsp. salt

Directions:

Begin by preheating the oven to 350 degrees Fahrenheit.

Next, peel and grate the sweet potato. Place the sweet potato in a mixing bowl, and toss the potato in the oil. Add the above dry ingredients.

Next, add the chickpeas to the food processor and process the chickpeas well. Add them to the mixture.

Next, mix together the flax and the water and allow them to sit together for thirty seconds. Add this mixture to the created mixture.

Add the rest of the ingredients, listed above, and create your 8 patties.

Next, place each patty on a baking sheet, and bake them for twenty minutes. Flip the patties and bake them for an additional fifteen minutes.

Eat the burgers however you like—with vegan bread and vegan cheese—and enjoy!

Mean Green Chickpea Creation

Recipe Makes 6 Servings.

Ingredients:

6 cups cooked chickpeas
2 cups chopped cilantro6 ounces chopped spinach
1 cup chopped onion

1 tsp. cumin
1/3 cup lime juice
3 minced garlic cloves

Directions:

Begin by processing the cilantro and the spinach together in a food processor. Next, bring all the above ingredients together in a serving bowl, and allow the mixture to stand together for ten minutes before serving. Enjoy!

Chinese Roasted Vegetable Bowl

Recipe Makes 3 Servings.

Ingredients:

1 chopped broccoli head
2 cups cooked chickpeas
1 chopped cauliflower head

1 tbsp. olive oil
salt and pepper to taste
1 tbsp. tahini

½ cup soaked cashews
2 tbsp. lemon juice

1/3 cup nutritional yeast
7 tbsp. water

Directions:

Begin by soaking the cashews for eight hours. Next, preheat the oven to 400 degrees Fahrenheit.

Next, place the broccoli and the cauliflower together on a cookie sheet, and drizzle them with oil. Next, place the chickpeas on the cookie sheet, as well, and bake the entire mixture for fifteen minutes. Afterwards, stir the mixture, and then bake the mixture for another fifteen minutes.

To the side, mix together the cashews, the tahini, the lemon juice, the water, and the nutritional yeast in a food processor. Pour this mixture over the roasted veggies and chickpeas, and season to taste. Enjoy.

Mapled Sweet Potato and Lentils

Recipe Makes 6 Servings.

Ingredients:

4 minced garlic cloves
3 cups green lentils
1 diced onion
1 diced sweet potato
1 diced apple
3 tbsp. maple syrup

14 ounces diced tomatoes
3 tsp. mustard
3 tbsp. molasses
1 tsp. salt
3 tbsp. apple cider vinegar

Directions:

Begin by boiling the water in four cups of water. Next, allow it to simmer for thirty minutes.

Next, preheat the oven to 375 degrees Fahrenheit. Add the apple, the onion, the garlic, the tomatoes, the sweet potato, the molasses, the mustard, the maple syrup, the salt, and the pepper to the lentils after they've cooked. Stir well, and add about 1 tbsp. apple cider vinegar.

Next, cover this mixture and bake it for twenty-five minutes. Remove the mixture from the oven, stir, and bake it for an additional twelve minutes. Add the other apple cider vinegar, and serve warm. Enjoy!

Layered Quick-Fix Bean Salad

Recipe Makes 5 cups.

Ingredients:

1 ½ cups chopped green beans
1 diced jalapeno
15 ounces chickpeas
15 ounces kidney beans

1 diced bell pepper
½ cup chopped parsley
2 chopped onions
salt and pepper to taste

Directions:

Bring the above ingredients together into a large serving bowl, and toss the ingredients to mix them well. Next, serve the salad with your choice of dressing, and enjoy.

Spiced Chickpea Burgers

Recipe Makes 8 patties.

Ingredients:

1 ½ cup uncooked chickpeas
3 minced garlic cloves
4 tbsp. sunflower seeds
1 ¼ cup cooked brown rice
1 diced jalapeno
1/3 cup diced red pepper

4 tbsp. BBQ sauce
1/3 cup minced parsley
1 grated carrot
1 diced onion
¼ cup panko breadcrumbs
4 tbsp. ground flax

Directions:

Begin by soaking the chickpeas overnight for nine hours. Afterwards, rinse them and simmer them for about fifty minutes in a few cups of water.

Next, Drain the chickpeas and mix them together with the other ingredients in a food processor. When you've sufficiently chopped the ingredients together, your dough should be sticky. Formulate patties from this mixture, and cook them in a skillet for about five minutes on each side. Enjoy!

Potato and Bean Salad

Recipe Makes 4 Servings.

Ingredients:

2 chopped red potatoes
1 diced onion
1 pound trimmed green beans
1 can cannellini beans
1 can red kidney beans
1 can garbanzo beans
1/3 cup red wine vinegar

3 tbsp. mustard
1/3 cup olive oil
salt and pepper to taste

Directions:

Begin by placing the chopped potatoes in cold water. Allow the water to come to a boil, and cook the potatoes for twenty minutes.

Next, boil the green beans. Drain them and place them in a bowl with the potatoes.

Next, add the rest of the ingredients into the salad bowl, and stir well to assimilate all the ingredients. Serve and enjoy!

Stunning Rosemary Red Soup

Recipe Makes 2 Servings.

Ingredients:

2 tbsp. olive oil
4 minced garlic cloves
1 diced onion
2 tsp. rosemary
1 tsp. rosemary

15 ounces red kidney beans
16 ounces diced tomatoes
1 cup vegetable broth
¼ cup water
salt and pepper to taste

Directions:

Begin by heating the oil, the onion, and the garlic together in a saucepan. Next, add the rosemary and continue to cook for two minutes.

Add the beans to the mix along with the vegetable broth, the tomatoes, the water, and a pit of salt and pepper. Mash up the ingredients well and allow the soup to simmer for seven minutes.

Next, season the soup with salt and pepper, and enjoy.

Quinoa Creation Chili

Recipe Makes 8 Servings.

Ingredients:

3 tbsp. olive oil
1 diced red pepper
1 diced onion
4 minced garlic cloves
1 tsp. coriander
4 tsp. cumin
2 tsp. chili powder
3 tsp. oregano
28 ounces kidney beans
15 ounces black beans

2 cups frozen corn
1 cup quinoa
1 cup of water
28 ounces diced tomatoes

Directions:

Begin by bringing all the ingredients into a slow cooker and cooking the chili for eight hours on LOW. Serve the ingredients warm, and enjoy.

Moscow Bean Salad

Recipe Makes 8 Servings.

Ingredients:

2 cans yellow beans
2 cans green beans
1 can red kidney beans
1 diced onion

½ cup apple cider vinegar
4 tbsp. parsley
3 tbsp. sugar
salt and pepper to taste

Directions:

Begin by rinsing the beans and bringing all the other ingredients together in a large mixing bowl. Stir well, and allow them to sit together for fifteen minutes. Next, serve, and enjoy!

Faux Noodle Chickpea Salad

Recipe Makes 3 Servings.

Ingredients:

1 ½ cup julienned cabbage
2 julienned carrots
1 sliced red pepper
1/3 cup chopped onion

2 julienned zucchinis
1 can chickpeas
1/3 cup chopped chickpeas
salt and pepper to taste

Directions:

Bring all the above ingredients together and mix well. Serve the salad with your choice of vegan dressing, and enjoy!

Mexicano and Chickpea Salad

Recipe Makes 4 Servings.

Ingredients:

20 ounces chickpeas
3 sliced onions
1 diced tomato
3 tbsp. olive oil

1 diced avocado
2 tbsp. lemon juice
½ tsp. chili powder
1 tsp. cumin

Directions:

Bring all the above ingredients together in a large serving bowl. Add the avocado just before serving, and enjoy.

Black Bean Revving Soup

Recipe Makes 6 Servings.

Ingredients:

2 diced onions
3 tbsp. olive oil
1 sliced carrot
4 diced celery stalks
5 tsp. cumin
6 minced garlic cloves

15 ounces black beans
1 tsp. red pepper flakes
5 cups vegetable broth
2 tbsp. vinegar
1/3 cup chopped cilantro
salt and pepper to taste

Directions:

Begin by heating the olive oil in a large pot with the vegetables. Cook for fifteen minutes.

Next, add the cumin, the garlic, and the red pepper flakes. Cook for one minute before adding the rest of the ingredients. Allow the soup to simmer for thirty minutes. Next, puree the soup in a blender and serve warm. Enjoy.

Chapter 12:
Vegan Pasta Recipes

Garlic and Tomato Penne Pasta

Recipe Makes 4 Servings.

Ingredients:

4 cups halved grape tomatoes
8 ounces penne whole wheat pasta
7 minced garlic cloves
3 diced shallots

4 tbsp. flour
3 cups almond milk
1 tbsp. olive oil

Directions:

Begin by preheating the oven to 400 degrees Fahrenheit.

Next, place the tomatoes in some olive oil, and slice them in half. Place them face-up on a baking sheet, and bake them for twenty minutes.

To the side, boil the pasta for about twenty minutes—until al dente. When the pasta is done, drain it.

Next, mix together the olive oil, the garlic, and the shallow. Salt and pepper the mixture and stir for five minutes.

Next, add the flour and continue to stir. Add the almond milk a bit at a time. Cook the mixture for five more minutes.

Next, bring the pasta, the tomatoes, and the sauce together, and enjoy!

Faux Veggie Macaroni and Cheese

Recipe Makes 3 Servings.

Ingredients:

12 ounces whole-wheat rotini
1 cup panko breadcrumbs
2 cups cooked broccoli pieces
1 cup diced potatoes
1/3 cup chopped carrots
1 cup water
1 tbsp. miso

¼ cup cashews
1 tbsp. lemon juice
1/3 cup nutritional yeast
1/3 cup vegan butter
1 tsp. Dijon mustard
1 tsp. salt
1 tbsp. tahini

Directions:

Begin by preheating the oven to 350 degrees Fahrenheit.

Next, cook the macaroni in salted, boiling water until it reaches its al dente state. Drain the pasta and set it to the side.

Next, steam the broccoli and set the broccoli to the side.

Next, place the potatoes and the carrots together in a saucepan with one cup of water. Boil this mixture for fifteen minutes.

Next, bring the final eight ingredients together in a blender, and blend the ingredients until completely smooth.

Bring the pasta, the sauce, the broccoli, and the other vegetables together in a casserole dish. Add the breadcrumbs overtop. Next, bake the casserole dish for thirty minutes, and serve warm. Enjoy.

Bursting Vegan Stuffed Shells

Recipe Makes 4 Servings.

Ingredients:

Vegan Ricotta Ingredients:
2 garlic cloves
2 cups cashews
2 tbsp. vinegar
2 tbsp. lemon juice

1/3 cup water
1 tsp. oregano
1/3 cup crumbled tofu
1 cup chopped kale

Shell Ingredients:

16 pasta shells
3 cups marinara sauce
1 tbsp. olive oil

Directions:

Begin by preheating the oven to 350 degrees Fahrenheit.

Next, puree the first eight ingredients in a blender or a food processor. Taste to adjusted the seasoning.

Next, bring this mixture into a separate bowl and set them to the side.

Place the shells in boiling water and cook them until they're al dente.

Next, pour a bit of marinara sauce in the bottom of a baking dish, and scoop filling into each of the shells. Place each of the shells at the bottom of the baking dish and drizzle marinara and olive oil overtop. Bake for thirty minutes, and enjoy!

Cauliflower-Based Fettuccini

Recipe Makes 4 Servings.

Ingredients:

5 diced cups of cauliflower
4 minced garlic cloves

½ tbsp.. olive oil
1/3 cup nutritional yeast

1/3 cup almond milk
½ tsp. onion powder
1 ½ tbsp. lemon juice

1 tsp. salt
dash of pepper
8 ounces fettuccine pasta

Directions:

Begin by placing the cauliflower florets in a pot with water. Allow the water to boil, and cook the mixture for eight minutes.

Next, add oil to the bottom of a skillet to sauté the garlic for five minutes.

Next, place the cauliflower, the garlic, the nutritional yeast, the almond milk, the garlic powder, the onion powder, and the salt and pepper together in a food processor. Blend the ingredients well to achieve a smooth sauce.

Next, allow a large pot of water to boil in order to boil the pasta for about twenty minutes. Drain the pasta.

Next, bring the sauce into the pot of pasta, and stir well, heating on low. Serve the pasta warm, and enjoy.

Avocado-Based Pasta

Recipe Makes 3 Servings.

Ingredients:

10 ounces pasta of choice
1/3 cup chopped basil leaves
3 minced garlic cloves
1 tbsp. olive oil

2 tbsp. lemon juice
½ tsp. sea salt
skin from 1 avocado
salt and pepper to taste

Directions:

Begin by cooking the pasta in boiling water until it's al dente.

Next, create the sauce by combining the garlic and the basil in a food processor. Next, add the oil, the lemon juice, the avocado skin, and a bit of water. Process the ingredients well.

After the pasta is finished, drain the pasta and bring it back into the large pot. Add the sauce and stir well over medium heat. Serve the pasta warm, and enjoy.

Walnut-Based Pesto Pasta

Recipe Makes 6 Servings.

Ingredients:

1 chopped head of broccoli
½ tsp. salt

15 ounces dry pasta
½ tsp. salt

½ cup sliced walnuts
2 tbsp. basil paste
3 garlic cloves
2 tbsp. lemon juice

1 tbsp. olive oil
1 ½ tbsp.. miso paste
2 tsp. apple cider vinegar

Directions:

Begin by boiling salted water and cooking the broccoli in the boiling water for three minutes. Afterwards, remove the broccoli and place them in cold water.

Next, add the pasta to the boiling water and cook for about twenty minutes. Leave half of the water in the pasta and drain the rest.

Next, combine all the last seven ingredients on the list in a food processor. Puree the mixture to reach your desired consistency. Afterwards, add the broccoli to the food processor, as well, and continue to process.

Transfer the processed pesto into the noodles with water, and stir well. Serve the pasta warm, and enjoy!

Orange Butternut Squash Sage Linguine

Recipe Makes 4 Servings.

Ingredients:

3 tbsp. olive oil
2 pounds diced butternut squash
1 ½ tbsp.. sage
3 minced garlic cloves

1 diced onion
1 tsp. red pepper flakes
3 cups vegetable broth
14 ounces linguine

Directions:

Begin by heating a skillet with the oil and the sage and stirring well. Next, add the onion, the garlic, the red pepper, and the squash to the skillet, as well. Season the skillet, and cook for about ten minutes. Add the broth to the skillet and allow the mixture to simmer for twenty minutes.

To the side, allow the pasta to boil in a pot until it reaches al dente. Afterwards, drain the pasta but keep one cup of water at the bottom.

Next, position the squash mix into a food processor or blender, and puree the mixture well. Combine this mixture with the pasta and the water, and cook the mixture for two minutes. Add salt and pepper if you like, and enjoy.

Ginger-Based Coconut Linguine

Recipe Makes 6 Servings.

Ingredients:

3 minced garlic cloves
1 tbsp. olive oil
3 tbsp. minced ginger
15 ounces dry linguine
2 tsp. vegan sugar

15 ounces coconut milk
3 tsp. lemon juice
salt and pepper to taste
2 cups spinach
1 cup swiss chard

Directions:

Begin by cooking the pasta in boiling water for about twenty minutes until you reach al dente.

Next, heat the olive oil in a skillet with the ginger and the garlic. Saute for five minutes. Next, add the sugar, the milk, the salt, the pepper, and the red pepper flakes. Allow this mixture to simmer.

Next, add the spinach and the swiss chard to the mixture, and cover the pot. Allow the mixture to simmer for seven minutes.

Transfer this creation to a food processor or blender, and blend the ingredients to create a nice cream. Stir this cream in the already cooked, drained pasta, and enjoy!

Vegan Prepared Alfredo Sauce

Recipe Makes 3 Servings.

Ingredients:

1 cup soymilk
¼ cup nutritional yeast
1/3 cup raw cashews
3 tbsp. vegan butter
4 tbsp. soy sauce
1 tbsp. tahini

2 tsp. Dijon mustard
2 tbsp. lemon juice
½ tsp. paprika
4 minced garlic cloves
½ tsp. nutmeg

Directions:

Begin by mixing the above ingredients well in a food processor or blender. Blend well, and enjoy with pasta or your favorite breads. Enjoy!

Chapter 13:
Roasted Vegetables and Other Delicious Vegan Sides

Green Beans with Grape Tomatoes

Recipe Makes 8 Servings.

Ingredients:

3 pints grape tomatoes
3 tbsp. olive oil

salt and pepper to taste
15 ounces green beans

Directions:

Begin by preheating the oven to 350 degrees Fahrenheit. Slice the tomatoes and coat them in olive oil and salt and pepper. Place them in a baking sheet, and cover them with foil. Bake them for sixty minutes.

Next, pour oil over the green beans and salt and pepper them. Place them on a baking sheet, and cover them with foil. Broil the beans for six minutes on high, and then toss the greens with the tomatoes. Enjoy.

Super-Delicious Vegan Gravy

Recipe Makes 4 Servings.

Ingredients:

1 cup chopped mushrooms
3 tbsp. olive oil
3 chopped sage leaves
1 tsp. white wine
1 tsp. thyme

4 tbsp. vegan butter
3 tbsp. flour
¾ cup vegetable broth
salt and pepper to taste

Directions:

Begin by heating together the mushrooms, the oil, the salt, and the herbs in a skillet. Cook the mushrooms for five minutes. Next, add the vinegar. Stir well for five minutes.

Next, turn the heat to low, and add the flour and the butter. Stir well until you've creted a sort of paste. Add the vegetable broth, next, to create a smooth mixture. Turn the heat up to high once more, and stir until you've created a gravy. If your gravy is too thick, you can add a bit of soymilk to reach your consistency. Enjoy!

Thanksgiving Cranberry Sauce

Recipe Makes 8 Servings.

Ingredients:

16 ounces frozen cranberries
1 cup sugar

1 ½ cup water
1/3 cup tangerine juice

zest from 1 tangerine

Directions:

Begin by heating together all of the above ingredients in a saucepan. Stir every few minutes. After fifteen minutes, the sauce will thicken. At this time, take the sauce off the heat, allow it to cool, and then chill it in the refrigerator. Enjoy whenever you please!

Stunning Steamed Asparagus

Recipe Makes 4 Servings.

Ingredients:

3 cups water
1 tsp. vegan butter

3 cups asparagus
salt and pepper to taste

Directions:

Begin by pouring water into a steamer. Add the butter, and bring the water to a boil.

Next, place the asparagus in the top of the steamer, and steam the asparagus for ten minutes. Enjoy warm with a bit of salt.

Mapled Carrots with Dill Seasoning

Recipe Makes 4 Servings.

Ingredients:

2 tbsp. vegan butter
4 cups sliced carrots
2 tbsp. chopped dill

2 tbsp. brown sugar
salt and pepper to taste

Directions:

Begin by placing the carrots in a skillet. Add water, and cover the carrots. Allow the mixture to boil. After the water evaporates, add the butter, the dill, the brown sugar, and the salt and pepper. Enjoy warm.

Electric Garlic Kale

Recipe Makes 4 Servings.

Ingredients:

3 cups kale
5 minced garlic cloves

3 tbsp. olive oil

Directions:

Begin by tearing up the kale leaves. Heat the olive oil in a skillet, and allow the garlic to heat in the olive oil for three minutes before adding the kale. Cook the kale for five minutes more, and serve warm.

Lemony Snicket Garlic Broccoli

Recipe Makes 5 Servings.

Ingredients:

2 chopped heads of broccoli
3 tbsp. olive oil
2 minced garlic cloves

½ tsp. lemon juice
salt and pepper to taste

Directions:

Begin by preheating the oven to 400 degrees Fahrenheit.

Next, toss the broccoli with the salt, pepper, oil, and lemon.

Bake the broccoli in the oven for twenty minutes. Add a bit more lemon juice, if you desire, and serve warm.

Super-Hot Red Cherry Tomatoes

Recipe Makes 4 Servings.

Ingredients:

1 tsp. sugar
2 tsp. vegan butter
2 tsp. basil

1 1/3 pint cherry tomatoes
salt and pepper to taste

Directions:

Begin by melting the vegan butter in a skillet. Add the basil, the sugar, and the tomatoes to the skillet, and cook them for forty seconds. Season them with salt and pepper. Next, cook the tomatoes until the tomatoes begin to blacken, and then serve the tomatoes warm. Enjoy.

Roasted Cauliflower

Recipe Makes 6 Servings.

Ingredients:

3 tbsp. minced garlic
1 chopped head of cauliflower

4 tbsp. olive oil
salt and pepper to taste

Directions:

Begin by preheating the oven to 450 degrees Fahrenheit.

Next, pour the garlic and the olive oil together in a large bag. Add the cauliflower to the bag, and completely coat the cauliflower. Next, pour this mixture into the baking dish, and salt and pepper the creation.

Next, bake the mixture for thirty minutes, making sure to stir after fifteen. Add some vegan cheese at the end, if you please, and enjoy.

Super-Sweet Sweet Potato Casserole

Recipe Makes 6 Servings.

Ingredients:

5 cups cubed sweet potatoes
2 egg substitutes
½ cup white sugar
4 tbsp. vegan butter
1 tsp. vanilla
½ cup soy milk

Topping Ingredients:
1/3 cup brown sugar
¼ cup flour
4 tbsp. vegan butter
1/3 cup diced pecans

Directions:

Begin by preheating your oven to 325 degrees Fahrenheit. Next, pour the sweet potatoes in a saucepan with water. Allow the water to boil until the potatoes are tender.

Next, mix together the sweet potatoes, the egg replacements, the sugar, the vegan butter, the soymilk, the vanilla, and the salt. Mix this together until completely smooth. Next, pour this mixture into a baking dish.

To the side, mix together the brown sugar and the flour. Add the vegan butter (for the topping) and the pecans. Continue to stir, and sprinkle this mixture over the created baking dish mixture.

Bake the sweet potatoes pie for thirty minutes. Enjoy warm.

Creamed Fall Corn

Recipe Makes 8 Servings.

Ingredients:

10 ounces corn
2 tbsp. vegan butter
1 cup vegan cream
2 tbsp. flour

2 tbsp. sugar
1 cup almond milk
1/3 cup chopped vegan Parmesan cheese
salt and pepper to taste

Directions:

Begin by heating the cream, the corn, the salt, the sugar, the butte,r and the pepper together in a skillet over medium heat. Continue to stir as you add the milk and the flour. Cook this mixture until the mixture is thick and the corn is cooked. Serve warm with a topping of vegan Parmesan cheese, and enjoy.

Zucchini Side Casserole

Recipe Makes 5 Servings.

Ingredients:

2 minced garlic cloves
1 sliced onion
2 pounds cubed zucchini
1 cup water
½ cup uncooked rice
3 tbsp. olive oil

2 tsp. garlic salt
2 cups chopped tomatoes
1 tsp. oregano
1 tsp. paprika
2 cups shredded vegan cheddar cheese

Directions:

Begin by mixing together the rice and the water in a saucepan and allowing it to simmer for twenty-five minutes.

Next, preheat your oven to 350 degrees Fahrenheit.

Pour the oil in a skillet and cook the onions, the zucchini, and the garlic for five minutes. Add all the seasoning, and then add the tomatoes, the rice, and the vegan cheese. Cook and stir continuously for five more minutes. Pour this mixture into a baking dish, and bake the casserole for twenty minutes. Enjoy!

Southern Living Collard Greens

Recipe Makes 6 Servings.

Ingredients:

1 pound diced collard greens
1 tbsp. olive oil
4 slices cooked tempeh
2 minced garlic cloves

1 diced onion
3 cups vegetable broth
salt and pepper to taste

Directions:

Begin by heating the oil and the tempeh together in a big pot over medium heat. After the tempeh becomes crisp, remove the tempeh and crumble it. Return the tempeh to the pan along with the onion, the garlic, and the collard greens. Cook this mixture for five minutes. Next, add the vegetable broth and the salt and pepper. Place the heat on low, and cover the pot. Cook the pot for forty-five minutes, and enjoy!

To the Side Roasted Butternut Squash

Recipe Makes 5 Servings.

Ingredients:

2 minced garlic cloves
3 cups peeled and cubed butternut squash

3 tbsp. olive oil
salt and pepper to taste

Directions:

Begin by preheating the oven to 350 degrees Fahrenheit.

Next, place the squash, the garlic, and the olive oil together in a large boil. Toss the squash, and then pour the squash into a baking sheet.

Cook the squash for thirty minutes in the oven, and serve warm. Enjoy.

Super Summer Grilled Zucchini Flats

Recipe Makes 4 Servings.

Ingredients:

3 length-wise sliced zucchinis
2 tbsp. olive oil

Directions:

Begin by preheating the grill to medium heat.

Next, drizzle the oil over the slices of zucchini, and grill the zucchini pieces on the grill for about five minutes per side. Enjoy!

Beautiful Table Acorn Squash

Recipe Makes 2 Servings.

Ingredients:

1 halved and de-seeded acorn squash
5 tbsp. vegan butter

4 tbsp. brown sugar
salt and pepper to taste

Directions:

Begin by pouring a bit of water in a microwave safe dish. Place the two squashes face-down in the water, and pierce the squash skin all over with a fork. Microwave the squash on high for twenty minutes, and then drain the casserole dish.

Next, salt and pepper the squash, and portion out the butter and the brown sugar in each squash half. Broil the squash halved for five minutes, and the enjoy warm.

Salty Squash Fries

Recipe Makes 4 Servings.

Ingredients:

1 halved and de-seeded butternut squash
salt to taste

Directions:

Begin by preheating your oven to 425 degrees Fahrenheit.

Next, slice the peel from the squash, and slice the squash into fry-like pieces. Arrange these pieces on the baking sheet, and bake the fries for twenty minutes, making sure to spin them over once or twice. After the fries become crispy, pull them out, allow them to cool for a moment, and enjoy!

Fried Green Zucchini

Recipe Makes 4 Servings.

Ingredients:

2 sliced zucchinis
1 sliced onion
1/3 cup cornmeal
½ cup all-purpose flour

½ tsp. garlic powder
1 cup olive oil
salt and pepper to taste

Directions:

Begin by placing the onions and the zucchini together in a medium-sized bowl.

To the side, mix together the cornmeal, the flour, the garlic powder, and the salt and pepper. Pour this dry mix over the zucchini, and shake the mixture well. Allow the zucchini to sit for thirty minutes.

Next, heat the olive oil over medium-high heat in a skillet. After the oil become shot, add the vegetables to the skillet and brown the vegetables evenly on all sides. Enjoy.

Glazed-Over Mustard Greens

Recipe Makes 4 Servings.

Ingredients:

1 tsp sesame oil
1 tbsp. sesame seeds
2 tbsp. soy sauce
1 tsp. sake

3 tsp. rice wine
1/3 cup water
7 cups mustard greens
2 tsp. minced garlic

Directions:

Begin by placing the seeds in a skillet over medium. Cook them until they're toasted. Next, add the seeds to a side bowl. Add the sesame oil to the skillet and heat this for two minutes. Add the greens, next, and the water. Stir the greens for two minutes before adding the soy sauce, the garlic, the vinegar, and the sake.

Next, allow the mixture to boil. Cover the skillet and allow it to simmer for fifteen minutes. Serve the greens with the sesame seeds, and enjoy.

Beans and Greens

Recipe Makes 2 Servings.

Ingredients:

2 tbsp. olive oil
3 cups kale
2 cups beet greens

15 ounces cannelilini beans
3 minced garlic cloves
1 diced onion

Directions:

Begin by heating the olive oil, the onion, and the garlic in a skillet for five minutes. Next, add the greens and cover the pan, leaving an inch of air. Allow the greens to wilt, Next, add the beans and cook the mixture for five more minutes. Serve warm, and enjoy.

Garlic-Based Spinach Side

Recipe Makes 4 Servings.

Ingredients:

10 ounces spinach
1 tbsp. vegan butter
7 minced garlic cloves
juice from one lemon
1 tsp. garlic salt

Directions:

Begin by melting the vegan butter in a skillet. Add the garlic and stir for two minutes. Next, add the spinach and allow it to wilt for five minutes. Lastly, add the lemon juice and a bit of garlic salt, and serve warm.

Creamy Tofu Spinach

Recipe Makes 8 Servings.

Ingredients:

12 ounces firm tofu
1 tbsp. butter
1 diced onion
½ cup soymilk

1 tbsp. olive oil
1 cup vegan Parmesan cheese
3 minced garlic cloves
2 pounds chopped spinach

Directions:

Begin by heating the olive oil, the onion, and the garlic together in a skillet. Add the spinach and allow it to wilt.

Next, mix together the vegan cheese, vegan milk, and tofu together in a blender. Blend until completely smooth.

Next, add the tofu mixture to the spinach, and cook the mixture until it's warm. Serve and enjoy!

Lemoned Chard

Recipe Makes 4 Servings.

Ingredients:

4 cups packed rainbow chard
5 tbsp. olive oil
7 minced garlic cloves

½ tsp. reed pepper flakes
1 ½ tbsp. lemon juice

Directions:

Begin by removing the stems from the chard.

Heat the olive oil in a skillet along with the garlic, the chard stems, and the red pepper flakes. Cook this mixture for three minutes. Next, add the chard leaves, and cover the mixture for five minutes. Stir and add the lemon juice. After three more minutes of stirring and cooking, serve the chard warm. Enjoy.

Fall Time Side: Apples and Sweet Potatoes

Recipe Makes 6 Servings.

Ingredients:

2 diced and peeled sweet potatoes
1 tsp. allspice
3 tbsp. vegan butter
1/3 cup white sugar

1 peeled and sliced apple
¼ cup soymilk
1 tsp. cinnamon

Directions:

Begin by bringing the sweet potato chunks together in a saucepan with water. Allow the water to boil for twenty minutes.

Next, melt the vegan butter in a skillet along with the spices and the sugar. Add the sliced apples to this mixture, and simmer the mixture, covered, for seven minutes.

Next, mix the apples with the cooked sweet potatoes—out of the water—and add the soymilk. Mix well with a fork or a mixer, and mash the potatoes well. Enjoy warm.

Thyme for Maple Syrup Sweet Potato Fries

Recipe Makes 4 Servings.

Ingredients:

1 pound sliced sweet potatoes
1 sliced parsnip
1 sliced carrot

5 sprigs of thyme
3 tbsp. maple syrup
olive oil

Directions:

Begin by preheating the oven to 375 degrees Fahrenheit.

Next, place the sweet potatoes, the carrots, and the parsnips together over a jelly roll pan. Add the salt and pepper and the oil. Toss.

Next, toss the ingredients into the oven and allow the vegetables to cook for thirty minutes. Place the thyme and the maple syrup over the vegetables, toss, and allow the vegetables to bake for twenty more minutes. Enjoy.

All Beet Up Sweet Potato

Recipe Makes 6 Servings.

Ingredients:

7 diced beets

3 tbsp. olive oil

1 tsp. garlic powder
4 diced sweet potatoes

1 diced onion
salt and pepper to taste

Directions:

Begin by preheating your oven to 400 degrees Fahrenheit.

Next, toss the beets with 1 tbsp. of olive oil, and spread this beet layer in a baking sheet.

Add the rest of the olive oil, the salt, the pepper, the garlic powder, the sweet potatoes, and the onions together in a plastic bag, and shake the bag in order to coat the vegetables.

Next, bake the beets for fifteen minutes. Add the sweet potatoes, next, and allow the mixture to bake for an additional fifty minutes. Make sure to stir every twenty minutes or so. Serve the mixture warm, and enjoy!

Super-Easy Applesauce

Recipe Makes 8 Servings.

Ingredients:

10 peeled and chopped apples
2 tsp. lemon juice
½ cup brown sugar

1 cup apple cider
2 tsp. cinnamon
½ tsp. salt

Directions:

Begin by mixing together the above ingredients in a large soup pot over medium. Allow the mixture to boil. Afterwards, allow the mixture to simmer for twenty-five minutes over low heat. Mash the ingredients with a potato masher, and serve the applesauce either warm or cold. Enjoy.

Currant is Current Applesauce

Recipe Makes 8 Servings.

Ingredients:

12 peeled and sliced apples
6 peeled and sliced peaches
½ cup herbal tea
1 tsp. ginger
4 cups red currants
1 tbsp. marjoram
½ tsp. allspice

Directions:

Begin by forming all the above ingredients except for the currants together in a large soup pot. Place the heat to medium-high, and cook and stir the mixture for thirty minutes. Next, remove all excess liquid. Add the currants, and stir well before serving warm or cold.

Primary Pear Applesauce

Recipe Makes 3 Servings.

Ingredients:

7 peeled and sliced apples
5 peeled and sliced pears
½ cup apple cider

2 ½ tbsp. cinnamon
1 ½ tbsp. sugar

Directions:

Begin by heating the apples, the pears, and the cider together in a large skillet for ten minutes.

Next, smash the fruit together with a wooden smooth, and continue to cook the mixture for thirty minutes.

Add the cinnamon and the sugar to the mixture at this time, stirring all the time, until it's completely cooked through—another ten minutes. Serve either warm or chilled, and enjoy!

Craving Craisin Bulguar

Recipe Makes 2 Servings.

Ingredients:

1 tbsp. vegan butter
½ cup dry bulgur wheat
1/3 cup craisins

1/2 cup water
2 tbsp. vegetable stock

Directions:

Begin by allowing the water to boil in a bot. Add the vegetable stock, the vegan butter, and the bulgur to the mix. Cover this mix, and allow the bulgur to simmer for twenty minutes.

Next, fluff this mixture and add the craisins. Season as you like, and enjoy warm.

South of the Border Mexican Quinoa

Recipe Makes 4 Servings.

Ingredients:

10 ounces diced tomatoes
1 tbsp. olive oil
1 ½ cup quinoa
3 minced garlic cloves
1 diced onion

1 diced jalapeno pepper
2 cups vegetable broth
1/3 cup chopped cilantro
1 store-bought package taco seasoning

Directions:

Begin by heating the olive oil, the quinoa, and the onion in a skillet over high heat. Next, add the garlic and the jalapeno pepper, and cook the mixture for three minutes.

Add the tomatoes, the seasoning, and the vegetable broth, and allow the mixture to boil. Place the heat on low, and allow it to simmer for twenty-five minutes. Next, add the cilantro, and serve warm. Enjoy.

Garbanzo-Based Quinoa

Recipe Makes 3 cups.

Ingredients:

2 cups water
1 ¼ cup quinoa
¼ tsp. salt
1 diced tomato
1 cup garbanzo beans

1 tsp. cumin
5 tsp. olive oil
4 tbsp. lime juice
2 minced garlic cloves
salt and pepper to taste

Directions:

Begin by bringing the quinoa and a bit of salt into a saucepan of water and allowing it to simmer, covered, for thirty minutes.

Next, add the tomatoes, the garbanzo beans, the garlic, the lime juice, and the olive oil to the mix. Add all the spices, and serve warm. Enjoy.

Pesky Pesto Quinoa

Recipe Makes 4 Servings.

Ingredients:

1 ¼ cup quinoa
2 diced tomatoes

3 cups vegetable broth
3 tbsp. basil pesto

Directions:

Begin by allowing the quinoa and the broth to boil in a saucepan. Next, cover the saucepan, and simmer the ingredients for twenty minutes. Remove the saucepan from the heat and add the quinoa and the tomato. Add salt and pepper as you please, and serve warm. Enjoy.

Garlic Mashed Potatoes

Recipe Makes 4 Servings.

Ingredients:

10 cubed red potatoes
3 tsp. minced garlic
3 tbsp. white sugar

½ cup vegan butter
1/3 tsp. garlic powder
½ cup almond milk

Directions:

Begin by placing the potatoes in a soup pot and covering the potatoes with water. Administer one tsp. of garlic to the water and allow the potatoes to boil for fifteen minutes.

Next, drain the water from the potatoes, add the vegan butter, and mash the mixture. Add the almond milk, the sugar, the garlic powder, and all the other garlic. Continue to mix the potatoes until you've created mashed potatoes, and enjoy.

Chived Vegan Sour Cream Mashed Potatoes

Recipe Makes 8 Servings.

Ingredients:

3 pounds quartered Yukon gold potatoes
½ cup soymilk
¾ cup vegan sour cream

1/3 cup minced chives
salt and pepper to taste

Directions:

Begin by placing the potatoes in a pot with water. Allow the potatoes to simmer for thirty minutes. Next, drain the pot and mash the potatoes with the rest of the ingredients. Utilize a masher or a mixer to get your desired consistency. Season the potatoes with salt and pepper, and enjoy.

Sweet Mashed Carrots and Potatoes

Recipe Makes 6 Servings.

Ingredients:

15 ounces baby carrots
1 cubed sweet potato
1/3 cup applesauce

1/3 cup vegan butter
1/3 cup brown sugar
1/3 cup raisins

Directions:

Begin by pouring the potatoes and the carrots together in a soup pot. Cover the vegetables with water, and allow the mixture to simmer for thirty minutes. Drain the mixture of water.

Next, melt the vegan butter in a saucepan, and add the brown sugar and the applesauce. Stir well. Afterwards, mash the potatoes and carrots together with the applesauce mixture and the raisins. Enjoy warm.

Cheezin' Potato Faux Pancakes

Recipe Makes 6 Servings.

Ingredients:

5 grated potatoes
3 egg replacements
½ cup soymilk
1 tsp. onion powder
½ cup grated vegan Parmesan cheese
1 cup flour

½ cup grated vegan cheddar cheese
1 tsp. baking powder
1/3 cup corn oil
2 tbsp. vegan butter
salt and pepper to taste

Directions:

Begin by mixing together the potatoes, the egg replacements, and the soymilk in a big mixing bowl. Add the vegan cheese, the flour, the onion powder, the baking powder, the salt, and the pepper. Stir well and assimilate with a fork.

Next, place the corn oil and the vegan butter together in a skillet, and heat the mixture well. Add 3 tbsp. of potato mixture to the skillet to make patties. Cook the patties for five minutes on each side, and drain them on paper towels before serving. Enjoy.

Easy Microwavable Baked Potato

Recipe Makes 1 potato.

Ingredients:

1 potato
1 tbsp. vegan butter
3 tbsp. vegan cheddar cheese

4 tsp. vegan sour cream
salt and pepper to taste

Directions:

Begin by place the potato on a microwave-safe place, and pricking it with your fork.

Cook the potato for five minutes on high. Turn the potato upside down, and cook the potato for an additional five minutes. Afterwards, slice the potato in the center, and add the butter, the salt, the pepper, and a bit of the cheese. Allow the potato to cook for one more minute to melt the cheese, and then add the sour cream. Enjoy.

Cashewed Rice Pilaf

Recipe Makes 12 Servings.

Ingredients:

1 cup wild rice
1/3 cup vegan butter
2 cups long grain rice
3 cups frozen peas
1 diced onion
4 ounces died pimento peppers

2 diced carrots
1 ½ cup golden raisins
1 cup cashews
4 cups vegetable broth
salt and pepper to taste

Direction:

Begin by placing the butter in a saucepan and melting it over medium. Add the long rice, the carrot, the raisins, and the onion together for five minutes. Next, add the broth and allow the mixture to boil. Then, cover the mixture and allow it to simmer on low for twenty-five minutes.

To the side, allow 2 cups of water to boil. Add the wild rice and allow it to simmer for forty-five minutes.

Next, add the wild rice, the pimentos, the peas, and the cashews to the raisined mixture, and heat on the stovetop at medium. Serve warm, and enjoy.

Broccoli and Rice Evening Casserole

Recipe Makes 10 Servings.

Ingredients:

16 ounces cubed vegan cheddar cheese
20 ounces frozen broccoli
4 cups instant rice
20 ounces coconut milk—without the water (just the cream)
1 cup water
1 diced celery
1 diced onion

salt and pepper to taste

Directions:

Begin by cooking both the broccoli and rice together in a saucepan, simmering the water for around twenty minutes.

Preheat your oven to 350 degrees Fahrenheit.

Next, mix together the cream of the coconut milk and the water. Add the cheese to the saucepan, and mix the ingredients together slowly over medium heat, allowing the cheese to melt. The cheese shouldn't burn.

Next, add the vegan butter to a skillet, and add the onion and the celery to the skillet, stirring all the time.

To the side in a mixing bowl, place the rice, the broccoli, the cheese mix, the onion, and the celery. Season this mixture with pepper and salt, and add the mixture to a 9x13 pan.

Allow the mixture to bake for fifty minutes. It should be golden-brown. Serve warm, and enjoy!

Chapter 14:
50 Vegan Dessert Recipes

Autumnal Pumpkin Cookies

Recipe Makes 12 cookies.

Ingredients:

1 tbsp. flax
3 tbsp. water
1 cup coconut sugar
½ cup canned pumpkin puree
2 tsp. vanilla
½ tsp. sea salt
½ tsp. baking soda
1 tsp. ginger
1 tsp. cinnamon

¼ tsp. nutmeg
1 cup oat flour (processed in food processor)
1 cup oats
1 cup almond flour
½ cup diced pecans
1 tbsp. arrowroot powder
3 tbsp. semi-sweet vegan chocolate chips

Directions:

Begin by preheating the oven to 350 degrees Fahrenhie.t

Next, mix together the flax egg with the water. Allow this mixture to sit for five minutes.

To the side, mix together the sugar and the pumpkin. Add the flax egg and the vanilla. Continue to stir. Next, add the cinnamon, the baking soda, the salt, the ginger, and the nutmeg. Beat.

Next, add the oat flour, the almond flour, the oats, the arrowroot, and the pecans. Stir well until you have a perfect dough.

Place this dough in a baking pan and spread it out evenly. Press the chocolate chips into the top of the cookie bar.

Next, bake the cookies for twenty minutes. Remove them and allow them to cool for ten minutes before slicing the squares and enjoying.

Trouble Chocolate-Chocolate Cookies

Recipe Makes 12 cookies.

Ingredients:

1 tsp. vanilla
½ cup cane sugar
1/3 cup brown sugar
1/3 cup sunflower seed butter
1/3 cup coconut oil
1 tbsp. ground flax
3 tbsp. water

2 cups oats (processed in food processor)
2 tsp. soymilk
½ tsp. baking powder
½ tsp. baking soda
1 chopped nondairy chocolate bar

Directions:

Begin by preheating the oven to 350 degrees Fahrenheit. Next, mix together the flax and the water in a big mixing bowl. Set this to the side for five minutes.

Next, add all of the first five ingredients to the flax seed bowl and stir well. Next, add the dry ingredients to the bowl. Stir well between each addition. Add the soymilk last to moisten the dough.

Chop up the chocolate and add the chocolate to the batter, stirring quickly.

Create dough balls and place the dough balls on a baking sheet. Press at them a bit, and bake them for thirteen minutes. Cool them for about fifteen minutes, and enjoy!

Oatmeal Cinnamon Bars

Recipe Makes 12 bars.

Ingredients:

1 tbsp. ground flax
3 tbsp. water
1 tsp. vanilla
1 cup coconut sugar
1/3 cup coconut oil
½ tsp. baking soda
1 tsp. vanilla

1 tsp. cinnamon
1 cup ground rolled oats (in food processor)
1 cup oats
1 cup almond flour
1/3 cup nondairy chocolate chips

Directions:

Begin by preheating the oven to 350 degrees Fahrenheit.

Next, mix together the flax seeds and the water and set them to the side for five minutes.

Beat together the sugar and the coconut oil with beaters. Next, add the flax egg and the vanilla and continue to beat. Add the soda, salt, and the cinnamon, and continue to beat.

Lastly, add the dry ingredients and beat the mixture until it's perfectly combined.

Next, spread the dough into a baking pan and layer the chocolate chips overtop. Press them into the pan.

Bake the cookie for twenty minutes. Afterwards, allow the cookies to cool. Slice them up and serve them. Enjoy!

Vegan Vanilla Almond Cookies

Recipe Makes 20 cookies.

Ingredients:

2 cups all-purpose flour
1 cup almond meal
½ tsp. salt
1 cup powdered sugar

1 cup vegan butter
½ tsp. almond extract
2 tsp. vanilla
20 almonds

Directions:

Begin by preheating your oven to 350 degrees Fahrenheit. Next, you mix together your dry ingredients in a large bowl. Add the wet ingredients, and stir well to create a dough. Don't add the almonds.

Next, roll your dough into a log with a two-inch diameter, and slice the cookie roll into flat cookies—like you would slice a cucumber. Place the cookies on a baking sheet, and press the almonds into the cookies. Bake the cookies for twenty minutes in the preheated oven, and enjoy.

Vegan Lover's Ginger Cookies

Recipe Makes 12 Cookies.

Ingredients:

½ tbsp. flax
2 tbsp. water
¼ cup vegan butter
2 tbsp. molasses
1/3 cup cane sugar
2 tbsp. maple syrup

1 tsp. cinnamon
1 tsp. ginger
½ tsp. baking soda
1 ½ cups light spelt flour
1/3 cup diced candied ginger
2 tbsp. sugar

Directions:

Begin by preheating your oven to 350 degrees Fahrenheit.

Next, bring together the flax and the water in a small bowl. Set it aside and allow it to thicken for five minutes.

Next, beat together the vegan butter, the molasses, the sugar, the vanilla, the syrup, and the flax mixture. Add the dry ingredients to this mixture and stir well. Lastly, add the candied ginger.

Create cookie balls and roll them in the 2 tbsp. of sugar. Place the cookies on a baking sheet, and flatten them a bit with your hands. Bake the cookies for twelve minutes. Allow them to cool, and enjoy!

French Lover's Coconut Macaroons

Recipe Makes 12 cookies.

Ingredients:

1/3 cup agave nectar
½ cup coconut cream
1 cup shredded coconut

½ tsp. salt
1/3 cup chocolate chips

Directions:

Begin by preheating your oven to 300 degrees Fahrenheit.

Next, mix together the coconut cream, the agave, and the salt. Next, fold in the chocolate chips and the coconut. Stir well, and create cookie balls. Place the balls on a baking sheet, and bake the cookies for twenty-five minutes. Enjoy.

Elementary Party Vegan Oatmeal Raisin Cookies

Recipe Makes 24 cookies.

Ingredients:

1 cup whole wheat flour
½ tsp. salt
½ tsp. baking soda
1 tsp. cinnamon
½ cup brown sugar
2 tbsp. maple syrup

½ cup sugar
1/3 cup applesauce
½ tsp. vanilla
1/3 cup olive oil
½ cup raisins
1 ¾ cup oats

Directions:

Begin by preheating the oven to 350 degrees Fahrenheit.

Next, mix together all the dry ingredients. Place this mixture to the side.

Next, mix together all the wet ingredients in a large mixing bowl. Add the dry ingredients to the wet ingredients slowly, stirring as you go. Add the oats next, stirring well. Lastly, add the raisins.

Allow the batter to chill in the refrigerator for twenty minutes. Afterwards, drop the cookies onto a baking sheet and bake them for thirteen minutes. Enjoy after cooling.

Classic Gluten-Free Cranberry Orange Muffin

Recipe Makes 12 muffins.

Ingredients:

2 ¼ cups oat flour
1 tsp. baking soda
1/3 cup sugar
1 tsp. salt

1 tsp. cinnamon
2 tbsp. ground flax
6 tbsp. water
2 tsp. orange zest

2 tsp. vanilla
1/3 cup almond milk
½ cup fresh-squeezed orange juice

1/3 cup melted coconut oil
1 ¼ cup craisins
1 cup diced walnuts

Directions:

Begin by preheating your oven to 350 degrees Fahrenheit.

Next, bring 2 tbsp. flax seed and 6 tbsp. of water together in a small bowl. Set this bowl to the side for five minutes.

Next, mix together all the dry ingredients. Afterwards, add the flax seed to the dry mixture along with the almond milk, orange juice, orange zest, and the vanilla. Administer the coconut oil at the end.

Gently mix the dough and then add the cranberries and the walnuts. Pour the batter into muffin tins, and bake the muffins for twenty-five minutes. Cool the muffins prior to serving, and enjoy!

Granola Grammar Muffins

Recipe Makes 16 muffins.

Ingredients:

1 cup granola
¼ cup oat flour
1 cup all-purpose flour
1 cup whole wheat flour
1 cup diced walnuts
2 tbsp. flax seed
6 bsp. Water

½ cup chocolate chips
1 tsp. baking soda
2 tsp. baking powder
2 cups applesauce
½ cup soymilk
½ cup brown sugar
2 tbsp. melted coconut oil

Directions:

Begin by preheating your oven to 400 degrees Fahrenheit.

Next, bring together the flax seed and the water and set them to the side in order to thicken.

Next, mix together all the dry ingredients. Mix the wet ingredients separately, adding the flax seed and water mixture after it has thickened.

Next, bring the two mixtures together and stir well. Pour the batter into muffin tins, and bake the muffins for twenty minutes. Allow the muffins to cool, and enjoy.

Revving Apple Parsnip Muffin

Recipe Makes 15 muffins.

Ingredients:

1 cup walnuts
1 cup grated apple
2 cups grated parsnip
2 tsp. baking powder
2 cups all-purpose flour
1 tsp. cinnamon
1 tsp. baking soda
2 tsp. vanilla

1 ½ tsp. ginger
½ cup raisins
1 cup melted coconut oil
1 cup almond milk
½ cup maple syrup
1 tsp. apple cider vinegar

Directions:

Begin by preheating your oven to 350 degrees Fahrenheit.

Next, grate both your apples and your parsnips.

Stir the dry ingredients together—everything except your apples and parsnips. Then, stir together the wet ingredients in a small bowl. Bring the wet ingredients into the dry ingredient bowl along with the apples and parsnips. Mix the ingredients until they're just moistened, and bake the muffins for twenty-five minutes. Allow the muffins to cool, and enjoy!

Careful Carrot Muffin

Recipe Makes 20 muffins.

Ingredients:

1 ¼ cup whole-wheat flour
2 cups bran flakes
½ cup coconut palm sugar
1 tsp. baking soda
1 tsp. cinnamon
1 tsp. baking powder
1 cup grated carrots
1 zest of an orange

½ tsp. salt
½ cup diced walnuts
1/3 cup raisins
2 cups almond milk
2 tsp. vinegar
1/3 cup avocado oil
1 tsp. apple cider vinegar

Directions:

Begin by preheating your oven to 400 degrees Fahrenheit.

Next, mix together all the dry ingredients in a large bowl.

Mix the wet ingredients together in a smaller bowl, and then add the wet ingredients to the dry ingredients, stirring slowly.

Next, fill the muffin tins with your batter, and bake the muffins for twenty minutes. Cool the muffins, and enjoy!

Crunchy Peanut Butter Muffins with Ginger

Recipe Makes 10 muffins.

Ingredients:

1 cup oats
1 cup flour
2 tsp. apple cider vinegar
1 cup hot water
1/3 cup crunchy peanut butter
1/3 cup canola oil

½ cup dark brown sugar
½ cup chunky applesauce
½ tsp. baking soda
1 tsp. baking powder
½ cup candied gingers

Directions:

Begin by preheating the oven to 400 degrees Fahrenheit.

Next, mix together the oats, the water, and the vinegar in a large mixing bowl. Allow the mixture to sit there for about twenty minutes.

Next, add the peanut butter, the oil, the sugar, and the applesauce to the mixture. Stir well.

Next, sift the dry ingredients together in a different bowl. Add this mixture to the wet ingredients, next, and stir well.

When you've mixed the batter, pour the batter into a muffin tin and allow the muffins to bake for fifteen minutes. After fifteen minutes, reduce the heat to 375 degrees Fahrenheit. Give the muffins another eight minutes. Next, remove the muffins and allow them to cool. Enjoy!

Lemon Ginger Bread

Recipe Makes 1 loaf of bread.

Ingredients:

1 ¾ cup whole wheat flour
½ cup sugar
1 tsp. cinnamon
1 tsp. baking soda
½ tsp. nutmeg
½ tsp. salt
½ tsp. cloves
2 tbsp. grated ginger

zest from two lemons
1 tbsp. olive oil
1 cup water
2 tsp. apple cider vinegar
For After Baking:
1 cup powdered sugar
juice from two lemons

Directions:

Begin by preheating the oven to 350 degrees Fahrenheit.

Next, mix together all of the dry ingredients. Afterwards, form two holes in the dry mixture. Pour the vinegar in one hole, and pour the oil in the other hole. Add the water, and then mix well.

Next, pour the created batter into a bread loaf pan and bake the bread for thirty-five minutes. To the side, mix together the lemon juice and the powdered sugar. Pour this mixture over the top of the bread after it cools, and enjoy.

Zucchini Chocolate Crisis Bread

Recipe Makes 1 bread loaf.

Ingredients:

1 cup sugar
2 tbsp. flax seeds
6 tbsp. water
1 cup applesauce
1/3 cup cocoa powder
2 cups all-purpose flour
2 tsp. vanilla

1 tsp. baking soda
½ tsp. baking powder
1 tbsp. cinnamon
1 tsp. salt
2 1/3 cup grated zucchini
1 cup nondairy chocolate chips

Directions:

Begin by preheating your oven to 325 degrees Fahrenheit.

First, mix together the water and the flax seeds and allow the mixture to thicken to the side for five minutes.

Mix all the dry ingredients together. Next, add the wet ingredients to the dry ingredients, including the flax seeds. Next, add the chocolate chips and the zucchini. Stir well, and spread the batter out into your bread loaf pan. Bake the creation for thirty minutes. Afterward it cools, enjoy!

Pull-Apart Vegan Monkey Bread

Recipe Makes 16 pieces.

Ingredients:

First part:
2 cups whole-wheat flour
1 tbsp. baking powder
1/3 cup sugar
1 tsp. salt
6 tbsp. vegan butter
Second part:
1 cup nondairy chocolate chips
1 cup soymilk

Third part:
1/3 cup sugar
2 tsp. cinnamon
3 tbsp. melted vegan butter

Directions:

Begin by preheating your oven to 350 degrees Fahrenheit.

Next, mix together the first part's ingredients. Cut the butter into the dry ingredients.

Next, mix all the second part's ingredients together into the first mixture. This should create a dough.

Next, create sixteen dough balls to splay in the bread pan. The dough balls should touch each other. Then drizzle the balls with melted butter. Mix together the sugar and the cinnamon, and sprinkle this creation over the monkey bread.

Bake the monkey bread for thirty minutes. Allow the bread to cool for a few minutes, and then eat up immediately. Enjoy!

Vegan Pumpkin Bread

Recipe Makes 8 Servings.

Ingredients:

1 cup gluten-free flour
1 cup brown rice flour
1 tsp. baking soda
¾ cup brown sugar
½ tsp. baking powder
1 tsp. salt
1 tsp. nutmeg

½ tsp. cinnamon
½ tsp. cloves
½ tsp. allspice
1 cup pumpkin puree
½ cup applesauce
3 tbsp. agave nectar
3 tbsp. water

Directions:

Begin by preheating your oven to 350 degrees Fahrenheit.

Next, mix together all the dry ingredients. Next, bring all the wet ingredients together in a different, larger bowl. Pour the dry ingredients into the wet ingredient mixture, and stir well.

Pour the batter into a bread pan, and cook the bread for fifty minutes. Allow the bread to cool prior to serving, and enjoy.

Banana Blueberry Bread

Recipe Makes 8 Servings.

Ingredients:

3 tbsp. lemon juice
4 bananas
½ cup agave nectar

½ cup vegan milk
1 ¾ cup all-purpose flour
1 tsp. baking soda

1 tsp. baking powder
2 cups blueberries

1 tsp. salt

Directions:

Begin by preheating your oven to 350 degrees Fahrenheit.

Next, mix together the dry ingredients in a large bowl and your wet ingredients in a different, smaller bowl. Make sure to mash up the bananas well.

Stir the ingredients together in the large bowl, making sure to completely assimilate the ingredients together. Add the blueberries last, and then pour the mixture into a bread pan. Allow the bread to bake for fifty minutes, and enjoy.

Creative Chocolate "Cream" Pie

Recipe Makes 1 pie.

Ingredients:

3 cups all-purpose flour
3 tsp. sugar
1 cup vegan butter

1 tsp. salt
8 tbsp. cold water

Filling Ingredients:

½ cup cornstarch
1/3 cup sugar
½ tsp. salt
3 tbsp. cocoa powder
1 ½ cup almond milk

1 cup coconut milk
1 tsp. vanilla
5 oz. chopped dark chocolate
8 ounces vegan whipped cream

Directions:

Begin by preheating your oven to 425 degrees Fahrenheit.

Next, mix together the flour, the sugar, and the salt. Cut the vegan butter into the mixture, making a sort of crumble. Add chilled water in order to make a dough.

Roll the dough out in the pie plate. Bake this pie crust for twenty-five minutes.

Next, mix together the filling ingredients: from the cornstarch to the vegan whipped cream. Mix well, and then cook the filling in a saucepan over medium heat. Stir continuously.

Next, fill the piecrust with the chocolate cream. Cover the pie and chill it in the refrigerator for four hours prior to serving. Enjoy!

Vegan Lemon Meringue Pie

Recipe Makes 8 slices.

Ingredients:

1 ½ cups sugar
1/3 up cornstarch
½ tsp. salt
½ tsp. agar

1 cup water
1 ½ cup coconut milk
2 tbsp. lemon zest
1 cup lemon juice

Meringue Ingredients:

10 tbsp. egg replacer
5 tbsp. chilled water

1 ¼ cup sugar
1 prepared pie crust (store bought)

Lemon Pie Directions:

Begin by adding the first group of ingredients: from the sugar to the lemon juice, to the saucepan. Allow the mixture to boil, stirring all the time. After it becomes very thick, pour the mixture into the pie pan.

Next, preheat the oven to 210 degrees Fahrenheit. In a separate bowl, mix together the egg replacer with the chilled water. Stir well, creating soft white peaks. Now, add the sugar. Mix slowly so that the meringue is super-thick and will refuse to fall down if tipped over.

Next, scoop this meringue over the chilled lemon filling, prepared above, and then allow the pie to sit for twenty minutes.

Now, allow the pie to cook in the oven for thirty minutes. Allow the pie to cool after baking, and serve. Enjoy.

Vegan Apple Cobbler Pie

Recipe Makes 6 Pieces.

Ingredients:

3 cups sliced apples
6 cups sliced peaches
2 tbsp. arrowroot powder
½ cup white sugar

1 tsp. cinnamon
1 tsp. vanilla
½ cup water

Biscuit Topping Ingredients:

½ cup almond flour
1 cup gluten-free ground-up oats
½ tsp. salt
2 tsp. baking powder

2 tbsp. white sugar
1 tsp. cinnamon
½ cup soymilk
4 tbsp. vegan butter

Directions:

Begin by preheating your oven to 400 degrees Fahrenheit.

Next, coat the peaches and the apples with the sugar, arrowroot, the cinnamon, the vanilla, and the water in a large bowl. Allow the mixture to boil in a saucepan. After it begins to boil, allow the apples and peaches to simmer for three minutes. Remove the fruit from the heat and add the vanilla.

You've created your base.

Now, add the dry ingredients together in a small bowl. Cut the biscuit with the vegan butter to create a crumble. Add the almond milk, and cover the fruit with this batter.

Bake this mixture for thirty minutes. Serve warm, and enjoy!

Vegan Vanilla Ice Cream

Recipe Makes 2 cups.

Ingredients:

3 vanilla pods
1 ½ tsp. vanilla bean paste
400 ml soymilk

600 grams light coconut milk
200 grams agave syrup

Directions:

Begin by slicing the vanilla pods and removing the seeds. Place the seeds in a big mixing bowl and toss out the pods. Next, add the rest of the ingredients, and position the ingredients into an ice cream maker. Churn the ice cream for forty-five minutes. Next, place the mixture into a freezer container, and allow the ice cream to freeze for three hours. Serve, and enjoy!

Vibrant Lemon Millet Cookies

Recipe Makes 20 cookies.

Ingredients:

1/3 cup olive oil
5 tbsp. vegan yogurt
zest from 3 lemons
juice from 1 lemon
1 cup flour

½ cup brown sugar
½ cup oats
½ cup millet flakes
½ cup unsweetened coconut flakes

Directions:

Begin by preheating the oven to 400 degrees Fahrenheit.

Next, mix together the dry and wet ingredients separately, and then bring the two mixtures together. Next, roll the cookies into twenty balls and place them on a baking sheet. Bake the cookies for fifteen minutes, and enjoy.

Vegan Strawberry Pie

Recipe makes 6 Slices.

Ingredients:

¾ cup raw cashews
1 cup oats
12 pitted and diced dates
4 tbsp. apple juice
3 tbsp. lemon juice
1 package firm silken tofu

1 tsp. grated lemon rind
1 ½ tbsp.. ground chia seeds
1 tsp. vanilla
2 tsp. agar powder
10 ounces sliced strawberries

Directions:

Begin by placing the cashews in some water and allowing them to soak for one hour.

Afterwards, place six dates in a food processor along with some oats. Next, add 2 tbsp. of your apple juice to the processor. This creates a sticky consistency. Press this creation into the bottom of your pie pan.

Next, add the cashews to the blender along with the rest of the dates, the tofu, the lemon juice, the chia seeds, the lemon rind, and the vanilla. Blend the ingredients until they're smooth.

To the side, heat apple juice and agar powder. Stir and heat the mixture until it begins to boil. Pour this juice into the blender and blend on high.

Next, pour this mixture over the piecrust, and allow the pie to chill for three hours in the refrigerator. Cover the top of the pie with sliced strawberries, and enjoy.

Vegan Pumpkin and Chocolate Pie

Recipe Makes 12 slices.

Ingredients:

1 cup canned pumpkin
½ cup coconut oil
1 cup cane sugar
1 cup all-purpose flour
1 tbsp. cornstarch

1 ½ tsp. vanilla
1 tsp. salt
½ cup cocoa powder
1 tsp. baking soda

Pumpkin Layer Ingredients:

1 cup canned pumpkin

1 tsp. vanilla

2 tbsp. arrowroot
4 tbsp. almond milk
1/3 cup cane sugar

2 tsp. cinnamon
½ tsp. ginger
½ tsp. nutmeg

Directions:

Begin by preheating your oven to 350 degrees Fahrenheit.

Next, mix together the canned pumpkin puree, the coconut oil, the cane sugar, the flour, the cornstarch, the vanilla, the salt, the cocoa powder, and the baking soda. Spread this mixture to the bottom of the pie plate.

Next, mix together the ingredients from the pumpkin pie layer. Add this mixture overtop the first layer.

Bake the vegan pie in the preheated oven for forty minutes. Allow the pie to cool and chill in the fridge prior to serving. Enjoy!

Vegan Chocolate Cake

Recipe Makes 1 Cake.

Ingredients:

2 cups all-purpose flour
1 cup sugar
1 tsp. baking soda
1 tsp. salt
½ cup cocao powder

1/3 cup canola oil
2 tsp. vanilla
1 tsp. white vinegar
1 ½ cups chilled water

Chocolate Frosting Ingredients:

5 ounces instant pudding mix
1 cup almond milk
10 ounces of vegan cool whip

Directions:

Begin by preheating the oven to 350 degrees Fahrenheit.

Next, mix together all the dry ingredients from the first ingredient list. Create a hole in the middle of the mixture and pour the wet ingredients into the hole, one by one. Stir the mixture, leaving a few lumps as you go.

Next, pour this batter into a cake pan and bake the cake for thirty minutes.

After the cake cools, prepare the pudding frosting by mixing together the cool whip, the pudding mix, and the almond milk. Stir well, and spread the frosting over the cooled cake. Serve, and enjoy!

Very Blueberry Morning Coffee Cake

Recipe Makes 9 Servings.

Ingredients:

1 ¼ cup whole-wheat flour
1 tsp. baking powder
¼ tsp. baking soda
¾ cup sugar
¼ cup applesauce
½ cup soymilk
3 tbsp. vegan butter

1 tsp. vanilla
1 tbsp. apple cider vinegar
½ tsp. almond extract
1 cup frozen blueberries
2 tbsp. brown sugar
½ tsp. cinnamon

Directions:

Begin by preheating your oven to 350 degrees Fahrenheit.

Next, mix together the brown sugar and the cinnamon. Melt the vegan butter in a microwave during this time, as well.

Mix together the dry ingredients in a large mixing bowl. Next, add the melted butter, the almond milk, the vinegar, the extracts, and the applesauce. Stir well, and allow the dry ingredients to become moistened. Add the blueberries last. Pour the ingredients into a cake pan, and spread the brown sugar and cinnamon overtop the cake.

Bake the cake for thirty minutes, and allow it to cool. Enjoy.

Good Morning Protein Pancakes

Recipe Makes 12 vegan pancakes.

Ingredients:

4 cups almond milk
3 tbsp. flax meal
1 tsp. vanilla
2 tsp. apple cider vinegar
3 cups all-purpose flour
1 cup hump protein powder
3 tbsp. sugar

1 tsp. baking powder
½ tsp. baking soda
1 tsp. salt
1 tsp. cinnamon
½ cup canoa oil
½ tsp. ginger

Directions:

Begin by stirring together the almond milk, the flax meal, the vanilla, and the apple cider vinegar. Allow this to sit for ten minutes.

Next, mix together all the dry ingredients. After the first mixture has curdled, add the canola oil to it, and bring the wet and dry ingredients together. Stir well.

Next, prepare a skillet with a bit of oil, and portion out about a fourth cup of batter out onto the skillet. Cook one side for about three minutes and then flip to cook the other side. Enjoy your pancakes!

Vegan-Inspired Coconut Cake

Recipe Makes 8 slices.

Ingredients:

2 cups shredded coconut
3 cups almond milk
2 tsp. apple cider vinegar
3 tsp. flax meal
1 cup toasted coconut flour
2 cups all-purpose flour

1 tsp. baking soda
4 tsp. baking powder
1 cup coconut sugar
2 tsp. vanilla
½ cup coconut oil
1 tsp. salt

Directions:

Begin by preheating your oven to 375 degrees Fahrenheit.

Next, mix together the almond milk, the flax meal, and the apple cider vinegar. Push this to the side.

In a different bowl, stir together the coconut flour, the bread flour, the baking powder, and the baking soda.

Next, mix together the coconut oil, the coconut sugar, the vanilla, and the salt. Add all the ingredients together in a large bowl, and stir well.

Pour the created batter in two cake pans and bake the cakes for thirty minutes. Allow the cakes to cool prior to frosting them with your favorite vegan frosting. Enjoy.

Upside Down 3-Level Apple Nut Cake

Recipe Makes 6 Servings.

Ingredients:

2 sliced apples
2 ½ cups all-purpose flour
1 tsp. salt
1 tsp. baking powder
1 ½ cup diced pecans
1 tsp. vanilla
1 ½ tsp. cinnamon
½ cup vegan butter

1/3 cup maple syrup
½ cup applesauce

Directions:

Begin by preheating your oven to 350 degrees Fahrenheit.

Next, prepare an 8x8 cake pan. Pour one tbsp.. of the maple syrup over the bottom of the pan. Next, add a layer of apples at the bottom followed by a layer of pecans. Utilize half of both.

Next, mix together all the dry ingredients in a separate bowl.

Add the wet ingredients to the dry ingredients, and stir well.

Add half of this created batter to the cake pan. Next, add another layer of apples followed by another layer of pecans. Spread the remaining batter over the pecans, and allow the cake to bake for fifty-five minutes. Allow the cake to coo for twenty minutes, and enjoy!

Home Made Vegan Peppermint Patties

Recipe Makes 25 patties.

Ingredients:

¾ cup cashews
4 tbsp. agave nectar
½ cup melted coconut oil
3 tbsp. almond milk

1 cup dark chocolate chips
1 ½ tsp. peppermint extract
1 tbsp. coconut oil

Directions:

Begin by soaking the cashews overnight in a bit of water.

Next, drain the cashews and place the cashews, the coconut oil, the milk, the agave, and the extract together in a food processor. Allow them to mix together until they're completely smooth.

Next, utilize mini cupcake liners in order to fill each with ½ tbsp. of the filling. Place the liners on the baking sheet, and freeze the fillings for thirty-five minutes.

After the freezing process, remove the patties from the liners, and place them back on the baking sheet. Allow the patties to freeze for an additional ten minutes.

To the side, melt together the coconut oil and the chocolate chips. Stir well, and allow the chocolate to cool for about three minutes.

When you remove the patties, dunk each of the patties into the chocolate mixture. Place the patties back on a piece of parchment paper, and freeze them for an additional ten minutes. Enjoy!

Groovy Christmas Time Peanut Butter Balls

Recipe Makes 20 balls.

Ingredients:

1 cup peanut butter
4 tbsp. maple syrup
3 tbsp. coconut flour

5 tbsp. rice crisp cereal
1 cup dark chocolate chips
1 tbsp. coconut oil

Directions:

Begin by stirring together the peanut butter and the maple syrup. Next, add the coconut flour. Allow this mixture to set for five minutes in order to firm up.

Next, add salt and the cereal, and create your small peanut butter balls.

To the side, place the chocolate chips and the coconut oil in a saucepan over low heat. After they've melted, dip each of the peanut butter balls into the chocolate. Place them on a piece of parchment paper immediately after, and allow them to freeze in the freezer after you've finished all of them. Enjoy.

Gluten-Free Chocolate Nubbins

Recipe Makes 24 balls.

Ingredients:

1 ¼ cup almond milk
1/3 cup olive oil
1 tbsp. apple cider vinegar
2 cups gluten-free flour

½ tbsp. vanilla
½ cup cocoa powder
1 tsp. baking soda
1 tsp. salt

Cake Ball Ingredients:

1 can coconut milk
1 package nondairy chocolate chips
2 tsp. coconut oil

Directions:

Begin by chilling the coconut milk. Preheat the oven to 350 degrees.

Next, stir together the milk and the apple cider vinegar. Allow this mixture to sit for five minutes.

Next, beat the vanilla, the oil, and the sugar into this prepare mixture.

Add all the dry ingredients into the wet ingredients, and portion the created batter into muffin tins. Bake these cakes for twenty-three minutes.

Next, allow the cakes to cool. Crumble the cake into a big mixing bowl.

Next, place the coconut milk in the mixing bowl a bit at a time, stirring all the time with your hands. Formulate 1-inch dough balls from this mixture, and freeze the cake balls for one hour.

Next, allow the coconut oil and the chocolate to mix together in a saucepan over medium heat. Stir all the time. Next, dip the created cake balls into this chocolate mixture, and allow the cake balls to cool once more. Store the cake balls in the fridge, and enjoy!

MM-Good Chocolate Macarons

Recipe Makes 12 cookies.

Ingredients:

1 mashed banana
½ cup maple syrup
1/3 cup coconut oil

7 tbsp. coca powder
1 tsp. vanilla
2 cups shredded coconut

Directions:

Begin by mixing together the mashed banana, the coconut oil, the vanilla, and the maple syrup.

Next, add the coconut and the cocoa powder. Stir well.

Scoop tablespoons of the batter onto a baking sheet, and place the baking sheet in the freezer for twenty-five minutes. Enjoy!

Faux Larabars with Chocolate Chips

Recipe Makes 12 bars.

Ingredients:

2 cups cashews
1 cup diced dates
½ tsp. salt

1 tsp. vanilla
4 tbsp. dark chocolate chips

Directions:

Begin by bringing the cashews and the salt together in a food processor to create the crumbs. Add the dates, and continue to process for about twenty more seconds. The mixture should be sticky.

Next, add the vanilla and the chocolate.

Place the created mixture on an 8-inch pan, and mash at it to make it level. Freeze the bars for twenty minutes. Next, slice them into twelve bars, and enjoy!

Better than Heaven Almond Butter Cups

Recipe Makes 12 cups.

Ingredients:

1 cup ground almond meal
2 tbsp. almond butter
1/3 cup ground oats
2 tbsp. coconut oil

2 tbsp. maple syrup
½ tsp. cinnamon
½ tsp. vanilla

Topping Ingredients:

4 tbsp. coconut oil
2 tbsp. cocoa powder

4 tbsp. maple syrup
½ tsp. salt

Directions:

Begin by mixing the oats and the almonds in a blender. Dump this mixture into a large bowl, and add the nut butter, the maple syrup, the coconut oil, the vanilla, the cinnamon, and the salt.

Stir the mixture well, and place the created mixture into the muffin tins. Press the dough down to keep it smooth.

To the side, mix together the coconut oil, the cocoa powder, the maple syrup, and the salt. Administer this sauce onto the muffin tin creations, and place the cups in the freezer for one hour.

Afterwards, serve chilled and enjoy!

Easy Vegan Chocolate Frosting

Recipe Makes 2 cups.

Ingredients:

Recipe Makes 400 ml coconut milk
1 bag non-dairy dark chocolate chips

Directions:

Begin by chilling the coconut milk, and then open the coconut milk, removing the excess water. Place the cream into the saucepan along with the chocolate chips. Melt the ingredients together on low heat.

Next, pour this mixture into a serving bowl and chill it in the fridge for twelve hours. After this time, you can whip the ingredients together to create a frosting.

Enjoy!

No-Bake Rockin' Roll Bars

Recipe Makes 16 squares.

Ingredients:

Bottom Layer Ingredients:

2 cups almonds
3 tbsp. coconut oil
2 tbsp. coconut syrup

2 tbsp. almond butter
1 tsp. cinnamon

Top Layer Ingredients:

2 mashed bananas
2 tbsp. almond butter

1/3 cup coconut oil
1 tsp. vanilla

Directions:

Begin by processing the almonds in a food processor. Next, add the remaining bottom layer ingredients to the food processor. Process the ingredients well to create a sort of "sticky" substance." Next, place this mixture into a baking pan, and push against it to push it down. Freeze this layer as you create the top layer.

Now, rinse out the food processor, and add all the top layer ingredients. Process the ingredients, and pour this layer over the crust. Allow the mixture to set in the fridge for two hours prior to slicing and serving. Enjoy!

Everything Raw Vegan Chocolate Fudge

Recipe Makes 24 squares.

Ingredients:

1/3 cup coconut oil
1/3 up almond butter
½ cup maple syrup
½ cup cocoa powder

1 tbsp. vanilla
1 cup diced walnuts
1 tsp. salt

Directions:

Begin by bringing together the coconut oil and the almond butter in a mixing bowl. Stir or beat well.

Next, add the cocoa powder, the maple syrup, the salt, and the vanilla. Beat the ingredients well until they are smooth. Add the walnuts last, and place the mixture in a bread loaf pan.

Freeze this fudge in the freezer for one hour prior to slicing and serving. Enjoy!

Chocolate Protein Balls

Recipe Makes 16 balls.

Ingredients:

1/3 cup hemp seeds
1 cup diced dates
1/3 cup sesame seeds
½ tsp. vanilla

1/3 cup cocoa powder
½ tsp. cinnamon
¼ tsp. salt
1/3 cup dark chocolate chips

Directions:

Begin by placing all the above ingredients together in a food processor. Allow the mixture to pulse into a sticky dough. Next, formulate small easy-to-eat balls and freeze the balls for twenty minutes prior to serving. Enjoy!

Coconut Craving Chocolate Bars

Recipe Makes 18 bars.

Base Ingredients:

1 cup almonds
1/3 cup coconut oil
½ cup oat flour
4 tbsp. maple syrup
1 cup rolled oats
½ tsp. salt
Middle Layer:
½ cup coconut oil
1 cup almond butter

½ tbsp.. vanilla
1/3 cup maple syrup
1/3 cup rice crisp
½ tsp. salt
Top Layer:
1 tbsp. coconut oil
1/3 cup dark chocolate chips
1/2 cup shredded coconut

Directions:

Begin by preheating your oven to 350 degrees Fahrenheit.

Next, mix together the crust, base layer ingredients in the food processor. The dough should be sticky. Press the dough in a baking pan. Bake the crust for fifteen minutes, and allow it to cool.

Next, stir together the oil, the syrup, the almond butter, the salt, and the vanilla (in the middle layer column). Allow the coconut oil to melt, and stir the ingredients well. Remove the mixture from the heat. After about ten minutes, add the rice crisp ingredient to the mixture, and stir well. Pour this mixture over the crust. Smooth the ingredients, and allow the mixture to freeze for forty-five minutes.

Afterwards, slicing up the bars and create the chocolate topping by melting the coconut oil, the chocolate, and the coconut together in a saucepan. Drizzle this chocolate over the frozen bars, and enjoy immediately.

Smooth Vegan Tapioca Pudding Recipe

Recipe Makes 4 Servings.

Ingredients:

2 cups almond milk
1 cup coconut milk
½ cup tapioca pearls
1 tsp. cornstarch

1 tbsp. water
1 tsp. vanilla
1/3 cup agave syrup
½ tsp. salt

Directions:

Begin by soaking the tapioca in 1 cup of the almond milk, and soaking the cornstarch with the tbsp. of water overnight. Next, add the additional cup of almond milk to the almond milk creation, and heat this mixture over medium. After it begins to boil, add the coconut milk, the agave, and the vanilla. Cook for fifteen minutes, stirring all the time.

Next, add the cornstarch mixture and the salt, and stir well for five minutes. Cool the pudding for about an hour before serving, and enjoy!

Avocado-Based Mousse

Recipe Makes 6 Servings.

Ingredients:

4 avocadoes
½ cup cacao powder
½ cup coconut nectar

2 tsp. vanilla
½ tsp. salt

Directions:

Begin by mixing together the above ingredients in a food processor. Chill the ingredients well in the fridge for three hours. Eat the mousse with fresh fruit, and enjoy!

Chapter 15:
Luscious Vegan Drink Recipes

Chocolate Creation Hemp Smoothie

Recipe Makes 2 Servings.

Ingredients:

2 ½ cups almond milk
3 pitted dates
3 tbsp. hemp seeds
4 tbsp. cocoa powder

1 frozen banana
1 tsp. cinnamon
5 ice cubes

Directions:

Begin by mixing all the above ingredients together in a blender, and pureeing them until you reach your desired drink consistency. Enjoy!

Non-Dairy Hot Chocolate

Recipe makes 7 Servings.

Ingredients:

1 cup soaked cashews
4 cups water
2 soaked dates
1 tsp. vanilla

1/3 cup cocoa powder
4 tbsp. agave nectar
½ tsp. salt
1 ounce chopped dark chocolate

Directions:

Begin by soaking the cashews and the dates together in a small bowl of water for two hours.

Next, bring these ingredients into a blender with the rest of the ingredients. Blend until you reach a smooth consistency.

Next, position this mixture in a saucepan and heat the mixture until the chunks of chocolate are melted. The cocoa should thicken. Serve hot, and enjoy.

Vegan and Healthy Christmas Cocktail

Recipe Makes 1 Serving.

Ingredients:

2 tbsp. vodka
½ cup cranberries
3 ice cubes
3 slices lime
½ tsp. agave

1 cup club soda

Directions:

Bring the above ingredients into a cocktail glass, and stir to combine. Enjoy!

Date with Cinnamon Smoothie

Recipe Makes 2 Servings.

Ingredients:

2 cups almond milk
1 cup pureed squash
5 pitted dates
2 tsp. cinnamon

2 tbsp. chia seeds
½ tsp. ginger
2 tsp. vanilla extract
6 ice cubes

Directions:

Bring all the above ingredients together in a high-speed blender and blend the ingredients well until you achieve your desired consistency. Enjoy!

Natural Vegan Energy Slurp

Recipe Makes 2 cups.

Ingredients:

2 ¼ cups coconut water
½ tbsp. lemon juice

2 tbsp. chia seeds
½ tbsp. maple syrup

Directions:

Begin by placing the chia seeds together with the coconut water in a large class. Allow this mixture to sit for fifteen minutes. Afterwards, add the lemon juice, stir the mixture, and enjoy!

Make Your Own Almond Milk

Recipe Makes 4 cups.

Ingredients:

1 cup soaked almonds
4 cups water
5 pitted dates

1 tsp. vanilla
½ tsp. cinnamon
½ tsp. salt

Directions:

Begin by placing the almonds in a bowl with water for eight hours.

Next, rinse the almonds and drain them out. Place them in a blender with the above ingredients. Blend the ingredients well, and then place a milk bag over a big mixing bowl.

Pour the blender mixture over the bag very slowly, squeezing it all out from the bag into the bottom of the bowl. This will take a little while.

Pour the milk back into the blender and continue to blend for about one minute on low.

Next, store the almond milk in your fridge for about one week, and enjoy.

Make Your Own Oat Milk

Recipe Makes 4 cups.

Ingredients:

1 cup oats
2 tbsp. maple syrup
2 ½ cups water

1 ½ tsp. vanilla
½ tsp. salt
½ tsp. cinnamon

Directions:

Begin by placing the oats in a large bowl and cover the oats with water. Soak the oats for twenty minutes. Next, drain the oats and rinse them. Pour the oats into your blender with three cups of water and blend the ingredients well, making sure to almond pulverize the mixture.

Position a sieve over a bowl and pour the milk into it, making sure to remove the chunkiness from your mixture. Pour the created liquid into the blender, and add the rest of the ingredients. Blend the ingredients, and chill the milk in a jar. Enjoy whenever you want!

Fall Time Pumpkin Pie Smoothie

Recipe Makes 2 Servings.

Ingredients:

¾ cup oats
2 ½ cups almond milk
1 cup canned pumpkin
2 ½ tbsp. chia seeds
2 tsp. cinnamon
½ tbsp.. molasses
1 frozen banana
½ tsp. nutmeg
½ tsp. ginger
1 ½ tbsp. maple syrup

4 ice cubes

Directions:

Bring all the above ingredients together in a blender and blend the ingredients until they're smooth, and enjoy!

Vegan Green Rough Rider Smoothie

Recipe Makes 3 ½ cups.

Ingredients:

¾ cup grapefruit juice
1 cup cucumber
1 chopped apple
1 cup kale
4 tbsp. hemp hearts

½ cup celery
¼ cup mint
½ cup mango
5 ice cubes

Directions:

Begin by bringing all the ingredients together into a blender. Blend them until they're completely smooth. Next, pour your green smoothie into a cup, and enjoy!

Conclusion

The past 365 days have been a whirlwind of health and wellness. All the appetizers, the cheeses, the sauces, the dips, the tofu recipes, the tempeh recipes, the seitan recipes, the bean recipes, and the desserts have fueled you to today: to a day with decreased disease, with smaller waistlines, and greater amounts of energy.

The vegan lifestyle yields a healthy, happy existence. Be happy you've made the choice to become vegan, to adopt all the wonderful recipes included in this book. Each recipe is pulsing with vibrancy; each recipe holds wonderful, exotic, and down-home ingredients: from garam masala to BBQ sauce. Bring yourself to continue to make good food choices, and naturally, you'll assimilate into a better lifestyle of good choices: from the way you exercise to the way you speak to your friends and family.

Throughout the vegan lifestyle, you've learned:

1. Whole foods—like natural grains, vegetables, and fruits, are key to longevity and overall health.

2. Animal products made you sluggish and a little smelly.

3. You find it easier to stick to your diet when you always have to prepare your meals ahead of time because you don't know who will be vegan where you're going.

4. You always make sure to eat enough protein in order to maintain your healthy muscles and retain your skinny waistline.

Enjoy your vegan journey!

Thank you again for purchasing this book!

Finally, if you enjoyed this book, please take the time to share your thoughts and post a review on Amazon. It'd be greatly appreciated!

Feel free to contact me at emma.katie@outlook.com

Check out more books by Emma Katie at:

www.amazon.com/author/emmakatie

Printed in Great Britain
by Amazon